Dedication

To all the single parents who make up at least a third of our population. You are doing the hardest job!

To my sweet husband, Donnie, you are without a doubt, God's choice for me. Thank you for your encouragement and patience with me.

To my two pillars and friends who walked alongside me during my 19-year single-parent journey.

Sande, God provided you in my darkest hours. Our friendship saved me thousands of dollars in psychological therapy. Thank you for the hours of reading and editing you so graciously provided.

Susan, God answered my prayer when I asked for a friend who'd walked this road. I thought you'd come with a map and could tell me how to be a single parent. Instead, I learned grace and strength from you. Your, friendship and wisdom are priceless. I miss you every day, but know that you're where your hearty's treasure always was.

Colleen, because of your encouragement, what began as a simple article has turned into a series of Marker books. You are the best cheerleader!

Brian and Bridgett, the two of you are the reason I kept going when it got too hard. I love y'all deeply.

Table of Contents

Markers for Single Moms:

Finding God's Direction in the Chaos

You have made known to me the paths of life; you will fill me with joy in your presence." Acts 2:28 NIV

Dear Single Mom,

This book was written just for you. I didn't write it so I could make money or become known in the writing and publication world. I wrote it to simply share with you about surviving in the world of single parenthood. A world I never thought I'd live in. As a young wife and mom, my comfortable world was uprooted and whirled into a directionless and chaotic state. When I put my faith and trust in Jesus Christ, He replanted me, setting roots deep into new ground and a new life with Him. It was in my brokenness and struggles that I came to know God in a new and intimate way. He opened doors that I would have never believed possible.

I want to share with you how putting your faith in this same Jesus Christ, who rescued me, can and will rescue you from wherever you are in your brokenness. A personal relationship with Jesus surpasses all human relationships. No matter what state your life may be in today, it is my desire that what I share with you will comfort you and bring hope where you may feel all hope is lost.

The word "Markers" in the title refers to those times when God reveals a powerful truth or moves on your behalf, resulting in a changed life and providing the direction you need. God will place these directional markers at exactly the time you need them, not too soon and not too late.

The idea for this book came after a hike up Arabia Mountain in Lithonia, Georgia, approximately 20 miles east of Atlanta. Arabia Mountain is a small granite mountain that is 940 feet high. I was in the middle of a crisis in my life, and had come there for solitude so I could think. I was desperately searching for direction from God and needed assurance that He was still with me.

My hike brought me to the highest point of the mountain where I saw an odd rock pyramid about three feet high a short distance away. When I walked over to it, I noticed another one some yards ahead. When I reached the second identical stone pyramid, I noticed a third one, but couldn't see a fourth one until I arrived at the third one. By this time I realized they were stone markers leading down the other side of the mountain. The interesting thing was I couldn't see beyond each marker until I approached the next one. In that moment, my mind and heart began making a connection between those physical stone markers and what God showed me next.

As I followed these stone markers, winding down the mountain path, God began showing me how He'd placed similar markers in my path all throughout my life. He began reminding me of major events He'd led me through and the impact those times left on my life. I felt His assurance that He was still with me and would guide me through my current crisis.

My curiosity, along with the markers, led me to the bottom of the other side of the mountain, where I found a small parking lot, a posted wooden trail map, and a small bathroom. This is where I was supposed to park my car and begin the hike, not on the other side, where I'd parked my car in the grass and had to fight my way through thick brush to get to the trail!

I laughed in spite of myself as I realized I had to hike back up the mountain and down the other side to get back to my car. I wondered how many times I'd gotten off path in my life because I didn't seek Him first for directions. I wondered how many times I prolonged something because I flailed around before simply coming to Him first.

The markers I am sharing with you in this book are some of my personal stories, as well as other single moms from the Bible and real life. All of these stories tell of an intimate, loving Father, who has our best interest in His heart that is above anyone else in our life.

My single-parent journey lasted 19 years. It began with a heart-wrenching divorce after nine years of marriage. The length of my marriage didn't lessen the impact of my life being suddenly forced in a direction I didn't want. After my divorce, I experienced some of the worst times of my life, but they were also some of the best times of my life. I witnessed God's personal involvement in such a way that, to this day, I can't fully explain. It's not because I'm someone special or more deserving. It is only because of my desperate cries for help and reliance on Him and His Word. I believe God cannot resist rushing to the aid of a single mom's cry for help.

It doesn't matter how you became a single mom. What matters is that you are searching for God's direction for your family and for you as an individual. In today's society, single parenthood has become common, but unless someone has walked that road, no one can truly understand the challenges you face daily.

When I was 23, I asked Jesus into my heart, which began my Christian journey. Several months later my husband followed suit. We found a small church to attend and jumped right in. Life was wonderful and I naively assumed our marriage was immune to the ravages of worldly temptations. Within four years, we were separated and headed for divorce. The gradual discovery of my husband's affair left me in shock, and after a year of separation, I filed for divorce. I was devastated. I found myself surrounded by broken pieces that I didn't have the ability to put back together. I entered the single-parent world in a frenzied, directionless state.

While the beginning of my new life started out rough, I learned about a Heavenly Father who met me in my deepest needs, right where I was. I learned how real He is and how He responds compassionately to those who cry out to Him. I became entirely dependent upon God to the point of reckless abandonment and trust in Him. This brought provisions and opened doors I would've never gone through had I not experienced bad times. He has taken what was meant for evil and turned it around for His glory!

Your circumstances may not be as drastic as mine or they may be ten times worse. Whatever your situation, God has a path planned for you. His way may seem too straight and narrow, but along that path you will find joy, comfort, peace and contentment. The other path is wide with many choices. It is the path of your way, where you will find temporary pleasures, loneliness, unfulfillment and danger, just to name a few. He is not going to choose for you or interfere with your will. My hope is that you will choose His way with a surrendered heart. If you do, you will experience a thrilling adventure that you could have never devised on your own.

Before we go any further, there are two things I need you to do. First, let go of the mindset that God won't do for you what He does for others. To think you're insignificant to Him is a lie from the devil. The second thing is surrender. Why is it that we women are so quick to surrender our hearts to an earthly man who can hurt and disappoint us, but we hold back from Jesus? Jesus loves unconditionally and will never leave you. As a matter of fact, Jesus is the man you are looking for! You can trust your heart with him. He won't break it.

Once you have done those two things, you're ready to move on. But let me warn you, if you have truly let go of that old mindset and surrendered your heart to Him, hold on because you may begin experiencing some feelings and attraction for the Lord that you didn't expect.

There is one last thing I want to clarify. I did not do everything right. I stumbled along the way and made many mistakes. It is by God's loving grace and mercy I'm even typing these words right now. God wants you to know He has a path planned out for you that is full of endless joys, peace, and contentment. It also includes sorrows and heartache, but the impact of those seasons will be lessened when you walk that path with Him and others. You don't have to walk alone.

It's my prayer that you will discover those markers that God has set in place especially for you. As you stay the course, I pray you are inspired and encouraged in your new life with Him.

Staying the course,

Terri

Marker One: Meet Jesus

The first marker God placed in my life was the day I accepted Jesus Christ as my personal Lord and Savior. It was at that moment of surrender when I finally quit resisting God's pull on my heart and said yes to Him. I said yes to being forgiven of all I'd ever done and would ever do. I said yes to Him coming into my heart to live through the Holy Spirit. I let go of all I'd thought I knew about God and realized I didn't know anything about Him at all. My need for justification, cleansing, and salvation was met when I accepted the gift of grace that Jesus provided through the shedding of His blood on the cross at Calvary. Finally, that bottomless space in my heart was satisfied!

Every human is born with an internal God-shaped space within them that only He can fill. This void in us seems to constantly grope for the nearest thing within our reach to fill it. Whatever we try to fill it with doesn't fit or eventually runs dry. The familiar emptiness drives us to search for the next thing to fill this void, only to find that thing doesn't fit either and leaves us empty again. It's one of those things that can't be fully understood. Once we accept Jesus by faith, something inside of us happens that is much bigger than anything else in life. When we make that decision, it's as if the blinders seem to fall from our eyes and our vision becomes clear and focused.

What I've observed and do understand is that when a person fills that void up with Jesus Christ, they stop looking. That's what happened to me. I stopped looking to fill that void over 27 years ago when I accepted Christ.

I was 23, married, and our son was two when I met Jesus. My husband had completed his three-year tour in Germany with the Army, and we had recently relocated to Lawrenceville, Georgia. I was working for a metal fabricating company where I shared an office with another young woman. I was quite a partier back then, as was she, so we became quick friends. It didn't matter how much alcohol I drank or pot I smoked, there was always a deep gnawing in me that indicated something was missing. My high times would bottom out with that familiar empty feeling that life was meaningless and the world was controlled by a mean and strict God.

My distorted view of God, who I wasn't sure even existed, was coupled with a paralyzing fear of what the future held. Rumors of nuclear war, terrorism, end times, and rapture of the church scared me. The thought of dying was something I just wanted to pretend would never happen. I went on with my life, as most people do, living in self-denial. My attitude was if I didn't think about it, I would never have to deal with the truth.

My new friend and office mate had an older sister who was telling her about Jesus and what the Bible had to say about all these issues that troubled me. My friend came to work every day sharing what her sister had told her about the Lord. We'd have discussions about current events and what the Bible had to say about all that was going on in the world. She brought pamphlets to work that her sister had given her that explained salvation through Jesus Christ and all the other issues we'd been talking about.

One day my friend came to work beaming, exclaiming something wonderful had happened to her the night before. She had accepted Christ into her heart and had experienced a huge lifting of burdens and knew she had been "saved." My first thought was, "Oh, great, now my friend is a fanatic," yet I envied her, too.

The next week while reading one of the pamphlets at home in my living room, I read I Peter 5:6-7. I read, "Therefore humble yourselves under the mighty hand of God, that He may exalt you in due time, casting all your care upon Him, for He cares for you" (NKJ). Those last five words "for He cares for you" grabbed my heart, and I let my guard down. Alone, there in my living room, I simply prayed, "God, if You are who you say you are, come into my heart and forgive me of my sins." He was faithful to that simple, prayer and has been constantly with me since. No matter how bad my life became or how good it was, the empty void had been filled. I experienced peace and joy in the midst of my pain and sorrow, as well as during the good times. I knew my future was secure with Him, and that life here was temporary, preparing me for an eternity with Him.

That moment in my living room was the first marker in my life with God, determining the rest of my life's direction. I didn't hear thunder or see bolts of lightning, but over the next few days, my heart was filled with indescribable joy. The fact that Jesus' Spirit could live in me to help me live this new life was great news. I knew where I stood with God and wanted to know everything I could about Him. My hunger to know Him, drew me to start reading the Bible and begin looking for a church.

Where are you with the Lord? Is your internal God-shaped hole filled with Jesus or something else? If you died today, do you know where you'd be? If you haven't entered into a personal saving relationship with Him, you're at your first marker with God that will determine your future now and for eternity. You don't have to know all the answers. He loves you passionately and desires a personal relationship with you. In John 14:6, Jesus said, "I am the way, the truth and the life, no one comes to the Father except through Me."

Today is the day of salvation, and He doesn't want anyone to perish. He is knocking on your heart's door right now. I hope you will accept His gift and enter into eternal life with Him. Only then can you enjoy the benefits of knowing Him. No religion, rituals or man-made path can put you in a right relationship with God. It's only through the Cross of Christ.

I heard a quote one time that goes something like this: I'd rather live this life as if there is a God you can have a relationship with through Jesus Christ, and enjoy the benefits of that for a lifetime, and die only to find out it isn't true, than to live this life as if there is no God, and then die, only to discover there is. After living in relationship with Jesus since 1983, I am fully persuaded that the second scenario is indeed reality. From Genesis to Revelation, the story of God's intimate relationship with all mankind is recorded. We have the free will to choose to believe or not believe. We can follow man-made rituals and doctrines, but miss the relationship with Jesus completely. Since that day in my living room, when I prayed my feeble salvation prayer, the constancy of God's relentless pursuit of me is what's kept me through the years.

If you want to make sure you belong to God and have Jesus live in your heart, all you have to do is pray a simple prayer like this:

> "Lord Jesus, I come to You just as I am. I don't understand all about You right now, but I have a void that nothing in this world will fill. I acknowledge that I need Your forgiveness. Please forgive me of all my sin and come into my heart today. I confess that You are God's only Son and that You paid the price for my sins. As You knock on the door of my heart, I open it to You and welcome You in. I pray this by faith in Your Name, Jesus. Amen."

If you sincerely prayed this prayer, you are born again and adopted into God's huge family of believers! Jesus said in Luke 15:10, "I tell you, there is rejoicing in the presence of the angels of God over one sinner who repents." They are celebrating with you! The first thing you need to do is get a Bible. A good place to begin reading is in the Book of John. If you aren't attending a church, start looking for one that teaches the Word of God, where you can settle in, develop healthy, supportive relationships and serve using your gifts and talents. Ask God to bring strong believers who will come alongside you, to encourage your new relationship with the Lord. You have begun a brand new life! Welcome to God's family!

"Therefore humble yourselves under the mighty hand of God, that He may exalt you in due time, casting all your care upon Him, for He cares for you" I Peter 5:6-7 (NKJ).

Marker Two: Dislocated? You Belong!

When I first became a single mom I felt hopelessly dislocated. Even though my small church family was supportive, they were mostly all married and really didn't know what to do or how to help. I didn't know anyone else walking this road. All I knew was this was not the road I wanted to take, but didn't have a choice. Events in my life were unfolding that were beyond my control. One day I was a married, stay-at-home mom with two kids, (six years old and fifteen months). The next day, I was separated, in desperate need of a job, and in shock over the events unfolding in my life. My heart was broken and I felt utterly hopeless.

What happens when someone's life becomes dislocated through divorce or a spouse's death? I remember my initial feelings were panic, fear of the unknown, hurt, anger, shame and despair. I had my life all planned out and that plan was dissolving quickly.

When a shoulder becomes dislocated, the arm just hangs, unable to function properly and needs support. Feeble knees can make a person feel lame and unable to walk straight. I imagine a dislocated shoulder is very painful, and I've seen people with bad knees and observed their struggles. If you have become dislocated from your life as you once knew it, finding yourself in a place you never dreamed you would be, you are not alone. There is hope.

Physical pain can be treated by doctors and medicine. Internal, emotional pain is more difficult to treat. There are medications to help with depression under the care of a physician. However, some people turn to alcohol or drugs to numb their pain, but it's still there, being further buried causing more harm. I have seen and lived through the devastation of alcohol and drugs and know that it's no answer for any hurt or pain.

Getting involved in a romantic relationship too soon after a divorce isn't the answer either; it's a recipe for disaster. You may think things will be different or better, not realizing that the baggage you brought out of the last marriage or relationship will come with you into the next. If you break your arm, it might need a cast and sling. If you break your leg it needs support. You don't go back out and start walking without a cast. If you go to the doctor to have a dislocated shoulder fixed or have joint replacement surgery, your body needs support and time to heal.

The experts say that for every four to five years of marriage, it takes one year to heal after divorce. The other heart-breaking truth about adults divorcing and jumping into new relationships is there are almost always children being dragged along with them in the process.

So what's a single mom to do when she finds herself in this place of dislocation? I felt I didn't fit in anywhere. I desperately needed God's direction, but didn't know how to find it. My life was in chaos. I didn't know how I was going to survive the mental and emotional strain, much less my newly acquired financial strain. My two kids needed me to hold it all together, so the only thing I could do was cry out to God. This was a struggle too, as I was angry at Him and didn't understand why He would allow the destruction of my family like this. Despite how I felt, I knew my survival depended upon Him. I needed something much larger and stronger than anything the world could offer me. I needed God more now than ever. That's when I started learning that not only could I survive, but I would learn to thrive.

My circumstances drove me to God's promises from His Word, promises of strong hands and knees, straight paths for my feet and assurance that I was unconditionally loved by Him. He showed me over time that I wasn't lame or dislocated, but that I belonged. He showed me He still had a purpose and plan for my life. The God of Creation is the God of second chances. No matter what happened, my circumstances didn't take God by surprise or catch Him off guard. He was as close as my next breath, waiting to provide the direction I needed.

Finding God's direction is a process that requires dependence on Him and belief that His promises in the Bible are for you. Whatever

He leads you to, you can be sure He will lead you through. He'll lead you to a new place of belonging and great sense of purpose and direction. The world has nothing to offer you in finding a sense of belonging, contentment and peace. Only God can provide this. Don't waste any more time trying to manipulate your life against the current. Find out what God has in store and enter His rest and flow.

There is a story about a single mom that has made an impression on me for years. She knew all too well what being a single mom was like and felt the pain of being abandoned and sent away from her home with nothing but a container of water and some bread. Her name was Hagar. Do you think she felt dislocated? Her story begins in Genesis, Chapter 16, and goes something like this:

Hagar was Sarah's maidservant. This meant she was held in high honor as the personal servant to someone with the status Sarah held as Abraham's wife. It also meant she was stripped of all her personal rights and subjected to Sarah's every wish. Even though Sarah had gotten too old to have her own children, God promised that she would still give Abraham a son. Sarah grew tired of waiting on God, and went ahead of Him, devising her own way to have a child. Have you ever gotten impatient with God about something and took matters into your own hands? I sure have.

In ancient Eastern culture it was acceptable to take a concubine in order to assure a male heir. Abraham and Sarah had been called out of this culture and set apart for God, so Sarah's attempt to secure an heir to Abraham was against what God had called them to do. In God's eyes it was polygamy, which has always been in violation of His design for marriage. Sarah told her husband to have sex with Hagar so she could get pregnant and they would raise the child as their own. Abraham went along with Sarah's plan and sure enough, Hagar got pregnant.

Soon Sarah got jealous of Hagar and treated her so badly that Hagar ran away. The Bible tells us that an angel of the Lord found her in the wilderness by a stream and advised her to go back to her position as Sarah's servant. God wanted Hagar to go back and face her problems. Maybe this was also His way of providing for her needs while she was pregnant. God also spoke to Hagar about what to name her son and let her know that He had seen her affliction. I think this encounter with God gave Hagar the strength to not only face her problems, but walk with confidence, knowing that whatever happened He would take care of her and her son. So Hagar went back and eventually gave birth to Ishmael.

God did fulfill His promise to Abraham and Sarah, and she eventually conceived and gave birth to Isaac when Abraham was 100 years old. When Isaac was old enough to be weaned his parents threw a big party. At the party, Sarah overheard Hagar's son mocking Isaac. It's possible that Hagar had grown prideful and fostered this unhealthy attitude in her son, Ishmael, due to the fact that he was Abraham's firstborn. Being the first-born male meant he would be heir to Abraham. This sounds like a modern day soap opera.

Once again, Sarah took matters into her own hands and demanded that Abraham get rid of Hagar and Ishmael to make sure Ishmael had no part in Isaac's inheritance. God instructed Abraham to do as Sarah asked and not to question the outcome.

Early one morning, Abraham gave Hagar a loaf of bread and container of water, and sent her and Ishmael away telling them to never come back. God's reasoning for this is beyond my understanding, but this was God's plan for Isaac to be of the lineage through which Jesus would be born. Can you imagine how Hagar must have felt as she walked out into the unknown? Ishmael was old enough by this time to know something bad was happening. I'm sure he also observed his mother's distress as they left the only home he'd ever known and headed into the wilderness. I wonder if Ishmael thought it was his fault. This seems so cruel, but even in this scenario God had a purpose for this single mom and her son.

The water and bread Abraham sent with them quickly ran out. In Hagar's mind, the only thing left to do was to sit and wait to die in the wilderness. Genesis 21:16 reads, "Then she went and sat down across from him (Ishmael) at a distance of about a bowshot, for she said to herself, 'let me not see the death of the boy,' so she sat opposite him and lifted her voice and wept." Can you imagine having nowhere to turn, nothing left to drink or eat, no direction whatsoever? Her hopelessness led to despair, to the point of death. Then she cried out to God and so did Ishmael.

The next thing that happened was a miracle. Verses 17-21 continues, "God heard the voice of the lad, then the angel of God called to Hagar out of heaven, and said to her, 'What ails you, Hagar? Fear not, for God has heard the voice of the lad where he is. Arise, lift up the lad and hold him with your hand, for I will make him a great nation.' Then God opened her eyes, and she saw a well of water. And she went and filled the skin with water, and gave the lad a drink. So God was with the lad, and he grew and dwelt in the wilderness and became an archer. He dwelt in the wilderness of Paran, and his mother took a wife for him from the land of Egypt."

What if Hagar had been too afraid to open her eyes when the angel of God spoke to her? What if she'd just sat there when she was told to get up? What if she didn't take the immediate resource she had and filled the empty water skin with the water that was provided and drink? God spoke, provided and she got up. If she hadn't followed the first direction, then the next, they would've died alone in the desert. When she obeyed the first direction, God must have then provided the next thing, then the next, and then the next because they survived and thrived.

I don't think Hagar had any family to go to for support when Abraham sent her away or she would've gone to them for help. She had no means of income and now a son to support with no help from anyone. The God of Creation, personally and intimately, came to Hagar's rescue and provided for her and her son. We see God's compassion, care and provision for Hagar and Ishmael. God meets her at her lowest point in life and provides a well of water in the middle of the desert! All we know after that is they both not only survived, but built a new life in a new place with new people.

It does not matter where you've been, what you've done or how you got to where you are today, the same God who rescued Hagar and Ishmael will rescue you if you cry out to Him in surrender. He sits on the edge of His throne waiting to hear from you, ready to meet you right where you are. "Yet the LORD longs to be gracious to you; therefore he will rise up to show you compassion. For the Lord is a God of justice. Blessed are all who wait for him" Isaiah 30:18!

The key here is surrender. That means to cease doing the same things you've always done. If you want different results, you can't keep doing the same things and expect your life to change. I discovered that I didn't have the power in and of myself to make the changes I needed. Surrendering your life to the power of the Lord begins the process of change. It's by His power, once you surrender to it, that you can make the choices necessary to redirect your life, change course and get on the path that He's already prepared for you.

My experiences were very different from Hagar's, but God always responded to my cries for help, some almost immediately, others took time. Whatever your circumstances, one thing I can tell you with confidence is that God hears your cry for help. As you trust, pray, seek and immerse yourself in His Word, you will find mercy and grace to help in time of need, according to Hebrews 4:16. "Let us then approach God's throne of grace with confidence, so that we may receive mercy and find grace to help us in our time of need." Approaching God's throne of grace sounds like a great place to start.

When you take God's word personally and allow Him to speak to you through His word, you'll experience deep joy and His direction for your life will become reality. Hagar's story is an example of God responding to a cry for help. What do you do when your children cry out? You don't ignore them, but respond. How much more does God in His perfect love respond to us?

When I first read Hagar's story I was amazed that God included so much about her. I was stirred and felt God's compassion for single parents. Even though I know God doesn't play favorites with any of His children, I'm left with the impression that He wants to reach deep into the lives of single parents and fill all the voids that a missing spouse leaves. God created the family unit and when it's torn apart, His heart breaks and He wants to step in. You're the only one who can open that front door and let Him come in.

It's hard enough to raise children with two parents in the same house. When one of them is missing, everything falls on you. Jesus said for us to come to Him. "Come to me, all who are weary and burdened, and I will give you rest. Take my yoke upon you and learn from me, for I am gentle and humble in heart, and you will find rest for your souls. For my yoke is easy and my burden is light" Matthew 11:28-30. How do we do this?

Oftentimes, when I'm weary and over-burdened, I mentally picture myself removing that big wooden yoke from my aching shoulders and neck. I'll say, "Here, Lord, you take this." I'm a visual, hands-on person and when I make this mental choice, it works for me. Letting Him take that yoke from you, may require putting yourself in a time out, taking some deep breaths and allowing these words He says sink in.

So where do you fit in? Being dislocated doesn't mean you don't belong anywhere. It simply means you need to be placed. God has a place for you and your family unit. How do you find where that is? Remembering this marker, that you belong, is the place to start. You may need new direction or redirection. Either way, God is going to show you, as you come to Him.

For years I carried the shame and guilt of my divorce. I felt that God had no use for me in His church family. I struggled with belonging anywhere. I continued to go to church, but most of the time, the smile on my face was a cover-up for the real pain I was feeling. If I had quit going to church I knew that I would spiral out of control out in the world, so I stayed "plugged" in.

Shortly after my divorce I left the small church I'd attended for several years and went to a rather large church to get lost in the crowd. I purposely went there to sit in a back pew without having to really connect with the people there. I did, however, have a few close married friends who supported me and encouraged me. Without them, I don't know where I'd be today. Back then I didn't realize the importance of staying connected.

I decided to check out a ladies' Sunday school class and discovered I wasn't the only single parent in the world. I met new people and made new friends. I didn't realize it at the time, but God was building a new support system around me. In time, God showed me that He had given me abilities and gifts that He wanted to use. By staying connected with a church family, Jesus rebuilt my life and my support system, one piece at a time. That's not to say I didn't make mistakes along the way, but His grace carried me through, teaching me how to rise above circumstances and mistakes to live a fulfilled life in Him.

Eventually I left this big church to help start a new church, which focused a lot on local and foreign missions. God used the horrible events I'd been through to give me compassion for hurting people, leading me to want to work with foreign missions. I was blessed with Pastor Mark, who didn't judge me by my history and what I'd been through. When I approached him about possibly leading our youth on a mission trip to Mexico, he saw beyond my broken life and encouraged me to move forward. I soared with encouragement that God could still use me and that there was a place for me in His church body. I began to see I was no longer a dislocated, divorced single mom, but a useful, vital part of the body of Christ.

If you have sincerely asked Jesus Christ into your heart and know that you belong to Him, you also belong in His church family. This is where you can build a support team around you. You will be as successful as the people you surround yourself with. You also have gifts and talents God has given you that He still plans on using. Your life may have changed, but it doesn't change the gifts, talents and abilities He has put in you. Planting yourself in a healthy church family is vital to finding direction for your life and using what He's given you. He wants to minister to you in that church family. He wants to teach you and grow your roots deep in Him, so He can also use you in His church and in your community.

God doesn't waste anything if we surrender all our circumstances to Him. He will turn them all around for His purposes and glory. You hold the key to unlocking that door though. Turn that key over to God and let Him have the last word, not your enemy, the devil! Take back from the devil what has been stolen and give it to the Lord, then watch and see what He does.

You belong to the Lord now. You have a place in His church and a purpose in His world-wide ministry. Come to Him with your weary hands and feeble knees. Let Him connect you and join you where you can heal and grow. You are a vital part of the Body of Christ, His church. He has planned some exciting and specific things just for you to do! He will take your wounds, scars, disappointments, sorrows, mistakes and use them for His purposes. That's just what He does and it's a slap in the devil's face every time we allow God to do this with our life.

"Therefore strengthen the hands which hang down, and the feeble knees, and make straight paths for your feet, so that what is lame may not be dislocated, but rather be healed" Hebrews 12:12-13 (NKJ).

Marker Three: You Have a Husband

Do you want a husband? You may be one who tosses her hair back saying, "Humph, that's the last thing I want or need!" Or you may be one who sighs, saying, "I want to be married." Maybe you don't admit it, but you secretly desire to be married or at least have a boyfriend. We all have different yearnings. No matter where your heart is in this area, every woman has a deep desire to be loved unconditionally. Even if the thought of being with a man is the last thing you want right now, the desire to be unconditionally loved is there. God placed that desire in us with the intent to fulfill it Himself.

I was twenty-seven when my husband walked out on me. My daughter was fifteen months old and my son was six. My husband was having an affair with my best friend at the time. We were all involved in our church, and our sons played little league baseball together. I was devastated. I wanted nothing more than for my husband to come back to me and for God to restore our family. When that didn't happen I felt forgotten and insignificant to God.

I heard about other marriages being restored. I personally witnessed God's healing power in a torn marriage as it was restored and became stronger than ever. I wondered why God didn't do this with my marriage. I believed the lie that I didn't matter, my kids didn't matter and my marriage didn't matter to God. I angrily expressed my feelings to God, "Well, I guess I just don't matter to you, do I? My kids are just not important to You, huh?" I'd struggle with reading about His promises and trying to hold on to them.

Then my pastor's wife at the time said something to me that changed my thinking. She explained it wasn't that my family and my kids didn't matter. While it is God's desire to restore and heal, He will never interfere with man's free will. My husband's free will is what was driving him to his destiny. I also had a free will to choose how I was going to live the rest of my life. She helped me realize that I still had choices.

I have never forgotten those words. I took her advice, held on to God's promises for me, and was able to take the first step of moving on with Him. I accepted that I couldn't change what someone else chose to do, and started realizing that God was much bigger than my problems. I had to take responsibility for my own relationship with Him and release my husband to God.

It wasn't easy. I can't tell you that the pain I was living in daily just dissolved. It took a long time, but eventually I began to heal. After a year of waiting, we were divorced. I struggled with longing for male companionship and wanting to feel desirable. I felt unlovely and unworthy of a man's unconditional love. I thought no one would want someone like me now. I'm damaged goods with two small kids. And how could I ever trust again? My negative thought life battled with the positive truths I discovered in my Bible, as I turned to God's word to find comfort and relief.

During the times I felt insignificant to God, I discovered Isaiah 40:27-31, "Why do you say, O Jacob, and complain, O Israel, my way is hidden from the Lord; my cause is disregarded by my God? Do you not know? Have you not heard? The Lord is the everlasting God, the Creator of the ends of the earth. He will not grow tired or weary, and his understanding no one can fathom. He gives strength to the weary and increases the power of the weak. Even youths grow tired and weary, and young men stumble and fall, but those who hope in the Lord will renew their strength. They will soar on wings like eagles, they will run and not grow weary, they will walk and not be faint." Now, read those verses again and insert your name in the place of Jacob and Israel.

When I felt unwanted and scared of the future, I stumbled on these truths in Isaiah 43:1-4 and inserted my name again in the place of Jacob and Israel. "But now, this is what the Lord says, he who created you, O Jacob, he who formed you, O Israel, 'fear not, for I have redeemed you; I have summoned you by name; you are mine. When you pass through the waters, I will be with you; and when you pass through the rivers, they will not sweep over you. When you walk through the fire, you will not be burned; the flames will not set you ablaze. For I am the Lord, your God, the Holy One of Israel, your Savior. I give Egypt for your ransom, Cush and Seba in your stead. Since you are precious and honored in my sight, and because I love you, I will give men in exchange for you, and people in exchange for your life.' " Wow! God is referring to the nation of Israel, but He uses His relationship with them as an example of what He wants with us. God used His word to speak directly to the raw pain in my heart and that's what He wants to do for you too!

Reading your Bible is vital to your healing and finding God's direction. It's also vital for deepening your relationship with Him, and dealing with life's constant demands. If you want God's direction and want to see Him work in your life, you need to spend time with Him. You need quiet time alone with God, to read His word, pray, talk to Him and be still and listen. You might be saying as you read this, that it would be nice to find five minutes alone to read and pray. I know all too well how hard it is when you have young children, and all the responsibility falls on you for everything. A lot of times, I longed to be alone with God, but was too exhausted at the end of the day to do anything but fall into bed. Mornings were too rushed. I felt I couldn't possibly get up any earlier. I'd hear how other people were able to fit it in and felt I wasn't trying hard enough.

I finally realized I couldn't fit myself into the same mold as others when it came to my personal time with God. Sometimes I struggled with knowing where to read, what to read, what to pray. Some days all I did was utter popcorn prayers on my way out the door like, Lord help me, watch over us, deal with this situation, rescue me, etc. Don't get discouraged if you can't block off the same time, every day, all the time. If life came at me so hard during the week that I missed out on my quiet time, I knew God was with me all throughout the day.

On my days off from work, or when the kids were at their dad's, I'd savor long, lazy mornings with the Lord. The laundry could wait along with my list of other chores. There were times when I was able to be involved in an in-depth group Bible study. A group Bible study is also a great way to hear from God, as He uses His word and other Christians to speak to you. This is what happened to me, as God placed this third marker in my life.

Several years had passed since my divorce. God had given me Sande, a new best friend, which surpassed anything I could have ever imagined to ask Him for in a friend. Our lives crashed into each other when I was still married, but separated from my husband. She had already trudged through the mud with me through some very difficult times and was now strongly encouraging me to join a weekly group Bible study with her called Bible Study Fellowship. This is a world-wide, interdenominational Bible Study that involves a nine-month commitment, requiring daily homework. My work schedule at the time allowed me to go. Sande lovingly told me I had no excuses and should join her in this study.

I wasn't very excited about it, especially when I learned the study was on Old Testament Kings and Prophets, which I felt was way over my head. Sande's persistence paid off though and I agreed to go. God used this group study to teach me so much that I wouldn't otherwise have learned. The greatest thing He showed me knocked me off my feet and changed my course of direction.

During this time I was struggling with wanting someone special in my life. I still had a lot of baggage and was in no way ready for a romantic relationship. I am so thankful that during this time God didn't allow me to meet any single men I found interesting, as I had huge trust issues. I still suffered feelings of shame, humiliation and abandonment. The last thing I needed was a boyfriend or worse, another husband. But it didn't mean I never longed for a romantic relationship.

One morning I was answering the weekly Bible study questions from Isaiah, Chapter 54. When I came to Verse 4, I read: "Do not be afraid; you will not suffer shame. Do not fear disgrace; you will not be humiliated. You will forget the shame of your youth and remember no more the reproach of your widowhood. For your Maker is your husband, the Lord Almighty is his name, the Holy One of Israel is your Redeemer, he is called the God of all the earth. The Lord will call you back as if you were a wife deserted and distressed in spirit, a wife who married young, only to be rejected, says your God."

I felt as if the Lord was talking directly to me. He'd just told me He was my husband! My husband's name is Lord Almighty! It then occurred to me that I would never be rejected by Him. He loved me no matter what and would never abandon me. He was my Maker, the God of the whole earth. My husband is the God of all the earth. I began to irreversibly fall in love with Jesus! I couldn't deny the words I'd just read and how they pierced my heart. It changed my life.

That was seventeen years ago at this writing. Even though I now have a wonderful earthly husband, Jesus is still my Heavenly Husband. I want you to know that you do have a husband and His name is Jesus. He's the perfect husband. He'll never say anything about your hair. He'll never notice your cellulite or care if you wear makeup. You might be saying, "That's great for you, but He can't physically hold me at night or hold my hand." While this is true, there are ways He meets your deepest needs that no earthly husband ever can, no matter how wonderful he may be. And if you want to find an earthly man, you'll be much better off letting your current Perfect Husband lead you to him.

This turning point brought me to a fresh, new understanding. I didn't have to guard my heart with Jesus. He understood me, without me having to explain anything to Him. We became inseparable. Someone once made fun of me and said that I used Jesus as a crutch, and hid behind Him. Well, of course I did! I don't know if crutch is the right word. More like Jesus was my complete support. Maybe hiding behind Him wasn't completely correct. I hid *in* Him and what a joy I found in that! That someone was my ex-husband. As I sit here today, many years later, I can emphatically declare that all the hiding in Jesus, with Him being my support, has more than 100 percent paid off and proven to be the absolute best thing I could have done!

During those times, when I went to church it seemed like I always sat in the pew behind a couple, and the man would end up putting his arm around the woman next to him. Sometimes I'd choke back tears. To add to that, there was always an empty spot next to me and I was sick of it. After realizing I did have a Husband, Jesus revealed to me that His arms were always around me. Deuteronomy 33:27 says, "The eternal God is your refuge, and underneath are the everlasting arms." Then one Sunday morning He spoke to my heart that the empty spot next to me belonged to Him. It was not empty!

When driving in my car He would hold my hand. "I, the Lord, have called you in righteousness, and will hold your hand" Isaiah 42:6. Now, if you just said to yourself, "I don't have that with Him," or "That's great for you, but...." then you need to go back to the beginning of the book and repeat steps one and two in my personal letter to you. There were always those times where I struggled and doubted. I would surrender something to Him, only to take it back. It was a constant process and still is today. He will get you beyond all of your doubting once you let go and allow yourself to fall in love with Him.

Do you believe Jesus died for your sins on that cross? Do you believe He lives in your heart now, through the Holy Spirit? Do you believe the Bible is the inerrant Word of God? II Timothy 3:16 confirms this, "All Scripture is God-breathed and useful for teaching, rebuking, correcting and training in righteousness, so that the man of God may be thoroughly equipped for every good work." If you believe this, then you should believe His words are for you.

In Mark Chapter 9, there's a story about a dad who brought his epileptic son to Jesus. He stood face to face with Him, asking Him to heal his son. In the last part of verse 22, the dad said to Jesus, "But if you can do anything, take pity on us and help us." In verse 23 Jesus replied, "If you can! Everything is possible for one who believes." Then in the last part of verse 24, the dad said, "I do believe; help me overcome my unbelief." I wonder where the mother of the little boy was. She may have been with him at home, but perhaps the dad was a single parent.

We established in Marker Two that you belong and are a part of the Body of Christ, his Church, the Bride of Christ. Now, let your Husband be to you all the things He desires. When you do that, you will feel and act like a different woman. You may not have the pain of divorce or a broken relationship. Perhaps you're a single parent because of adoption. You may still deal with loneliness and the desire for a male companion or even marriage. While God may certainly bring that future mate to you, He will be your Heavenly Husband forever.

I have one last story to share with you about our Husband, Jesus, so you will know how intimate and personal He wants to be with you. I had finally met someone I was very interested in about 10 years after my divorce. We became good friends. After over a year of getting to know each other and working together with the church youth, we eventually started dating and fell in love. I was so sure he was the one. He was a wonderful godly man, but things didn't work out for various reasons. The main thing I learned from that relationship is that you can never put God on the back burner and allow any man to become more important than God. I did that. Once again, I was heartbroken.

A couple years after our break up, I had to go out of town for my job. It was on the Georgia coast, so I made arrangements to take a couple days off from work and make a long weekend out of it. I reserved a room for three nights on Jekyll Island, and made plans to take the ferry to nearby Cumberland Island on my second day. Cumberland Island is a small, unspoiled barrier island about 45 minutes from Jekyl Island. No one lives there. There is just one small Inn to stay, but no hotels. Wild horses and other wildlife roam freely among old ruins and beautiful walking trails. I couldn't wait to be alone for some peace and quiet and see the island. I'm a sucker for a little adventure.

I arrived on Jekyll Island excited about my plans for my long weekend getaway alone. I was going to rest, lay on the beach, read, journal and take long walks. By the end of my first day there, I was unexpectedly overcome with loneliness. I felt isolated and forgotten. There was this terrible ache in my heart for companionship that I couldn't shake. It came on suddenly and I'd never felt it this strongly before. It was terrible!

On the second day I made the 45-minute drive in pouring rain to St. Mary's. St. Mary's is a small, quaint fishing town located on St. Mary's River that feeds into the Atlantic Ocean. This is where I was to catch the ferry that would take me to Cumberland Island. Due to the rain and traffic, I was late and missed the first ferry. The next one wouldn't leave for an hour and a half. The rain had turned into a light mist, so while I waited, I walked along the sidewalk-framed streets. The streets were lined with proudly displayed, renovated Victorian-style homes and Inns. Huge live-oak trees provided a canopy over some of the streets, acting as an umbrella from the mist. It was beautiful and I longed to be able to share this time with someone special.

I suddenly remembered that my ex-boyfriend and I had talked about coming there together to explore Cumberland Island. My loneliness intensified and all I could do was cry. I suddenly wished he'd come walking down the street so we could do this together. The cloudy, misty weather dampened my state of mind and the loneliness became overwhelming.

Eventually I returned back to the dock where I would catch the ferry. I sat down in a nearby courtyard on a white bench swing. As I sat there wallowing in self-pity, I thought I felt something lightly touch me on my left shoulder. It felt so real that I turned around expecting someone to be standing there. When I turned and looked, there was a fresh, single red rose resting on a piece of the swing right next to my left shoulder. I looked around for a rose bush, but there was not one in sight anywhere. It was still misting so I was the only person in the courtyard. I knew it was somehow from the Lord, and He wanted me to know He knew my heart ached and He was there. The loneliness lifted as I caught the ferry, and enjoyed my day on Cumberland Island.

In sharing these stories with you, it has caused me to re-evaluate my relationship with the Lord today. I so easily forget all these things He has done. Remembering them reminds me that the Lord Jesus is still my spiritual Husband, first and foremost. Then my earthly husband is next on the priority list. I haven't always walked that closely with Jesus throughout all these years, but wish I would have. It's true what is said that God never shifts or moves away from us in our relationship with Him. It's we who move from Him. I am so glad He's faithful and never stops His relentless pursuit of me. He pursues us like no earthly man ever will.

He's pursuing you right now. He has planned so much for you and your life with Him. Don't miss out on the romance story that belongs to you. Your love story can begin at Isaiah 54:4. Or you may have a different beginning. Live your story with the Lord, so you can one day tell it to someone else.

"For your Maker is your husband, the Lord of hosts is His name, and your Redeemer is the Holy One of Israel, He is called the God of the whole earth," Isaiah 54:5 (NKJ).

Marker Four: Standing at the Crossroads

When we're on a road trip or driving in unfamiliar territory, we usually have a road map or written directions. We also look for landmarks and mile markers. These days, we all mostly use some type of GPS or Google maps on our phones. The voice will instruct us as we're driving, "turn right, turn left" or "drive on the highlighted route," mapping out your destination. It will even recalculate for you if you make a wrong turn.

Wouldn't it be wonderful if God would do that every time we needed an answer when facing decisions, or recalculate when we make mistakes? But there are numerous ways God does speak to us and show us which way to go. Life is full of twists and turns, and God will not leave you out there to get lost. Jesus longs to speak to you and provide direction.

Some women have told me God doesn't speak to them. I don't buy that. He doesn't pick and choose who is able to hear from Him. The other question I hear a lot is, "How can you know when it's really God's voice you hear?" I'm going to share my own journey in becoming familiar with God's voice and what I learned through the process. I hope you are encouraged as you seek Him for direction in your own life or a major decision you're facing.

Jesus is the Shepherd and we are his sheep. "When he brings out his own sheep, he goes before them, and the sheep follow him, for they know his voice" John 10:4 (NKJ). Jesus used the relationship between a shepherd and his sheep as an example for us. A herd of sheep will never follow a stranger. The only voice they recognize is their shepherd. In John 18:37 when Jesus stood before Pilate, He said, "Everyone who is of the truth hears My voice" (NKJ). If sheep, which are known as dumb animals, can recognize their shepherd's voice, be encouraged that you can know God's voice too.

Knowing God's voice isn't a super-spiritual quality that some Christians have and others don't. It does, however, depend on time spent with God regularly and your awareness of His presence in your life. Your children know your voice and you know theirs. It comes naturally. After a while, hearing and knowing God's voice will come naturally to you too.

The challenges of being a single parent can make you feel like your life is one decision-making event after another. There are times you face pressing decisions and feel you can't take the time to wait for God's direction or sit down long enough to get quiet before Him to hear His voice. This is when you can't afford NOT to get quiet with Him and simply ask, "Lord, what would You have me do in this situation?"

For a long time it seemed my life was consumed by one decision-making trial after another. I grew weary of making decisions alone and longed for a break. I looked at families with two parents and envied them, thinking how much easier they had it, and I'd feel sorry for myself. But I learned that often what may be perceived by outsiders is not always the reality in other families. Our imaginations can lie to us and comparing your life with someone else's will hinder what God has for you.

When life pulls you in different directions, sometimes you need to take a timeout. It may be a 30-minute timeout, one-day timeout or a whole weekend. If you're finding there's no time for a little peace and quiet in your schedule, then maybe it's time to look at all your involvements, including the kids' schedules. I used to have a problem with being able to say "no". I also had a problem with getting involved in too many causes, good causes, but not when it interferes with other obligations and priorities.

It didn't take long for me to discover the bliss of quiet time with the Lord. It was at that place where He would minister to my heart, reveal things to me in His word or provide direction. If the laundry didn't get put away, at least we had clean clothes. The unorganized closest or dirty car could wait another day or even another week. I relied on that time with God to enable me to get through my days.

When my kids were gone for the weekend, I took advantage of the time alone to go somewhere by myself. It might be for a few hours or a whole day. I would leave my home so I wouldn't do housework, yard work, or whatever other work demanded my attention. Sometimes I'd take a long brisk walk or grab my Bible and a notebook and just leave for a while. I had a few favorite outdoor spots where I could relax. I made sure it was a safe public spot with people around, but secluded enough for peace and quiet. If ten minutes is all you can grab, ten minutes of solitude with God will amazingly affect how the next ten hours will unfold.

In Isaiah 30:19-21 we read, "O people of Zion, who live in Jerusalem, you will weep no more. How gracious He will be when you cry for help! As soon as He hears, He will answer you. Although the Lord gives you the bread of adversity and water of affliction, your teachers will be hidden no more; with your own eyes you will see them. Whether you turn to the right or to the left, your ears will hear a voice behind you, saying, 'This is the way; walk in it.' " Be encouraged, take heart! There is hope that you will see the end of your adversity. Cry out to the Lord and in His grace He will hear you and answer. He promises that even though these things were allowed into your life, He will walk through them with you and you will learn much from Him.

The Lord doesn't cause problems and trials in our lives, but He does allow them with a purpose in mind. One thing I'm sure of is that He keeps His promise to walk through these times with us. He is right there, like a heavenly GPS saying, "This is the way; walk in it."

After I'd been single for a few years, there were many times I was glad I didn't have the distraction of a mate, (especially when I was reminded that husbands and wives do bicker). As you focus more on what God says, soon you will sense a peaceful, quiet voice saying, "Go this way, turn here, follow Me."

Whatever the magnitude of your crossroad today, invite God in on your decision-making. It may be as simple as asking, "Lord, what would You do?" Then be quiet a moment and see what happens. Sometimes nothing will happen and I take that to mean, don't do anything just yet. Your decision for today may just be to follow God more closely, which is a wonderful one to make.

Many times when I've been praying, looking for answers, I would feel a tug at my heart or sense something in my heart and mind that wouldn't normally be there. I'd ask, "Is that You, Lord?" To make sure it was Him, I'd ask myself if it lined up with His word or did it require an action that would be in line with His word. Sometimes it was just Him speaking simple truths to my heart or gently showing me a behavior I needed to get rid of.

About five years after my divorce, the Lord brought me to a very exciting crossroads. It required making some major decisions that would greatly affect both mine and my children's lives. The decision to continue onward where I felt God's leading required us to move away for several months. It was wild, adventurous and absolutely impossible for me to do on my own. It didn't make any sense in the world's eyes.

It first began at a home Bible study for singles that I attended weekly. One night, two men visiting our group had recently returned from a short-term mission trip. They shared pictures and stories that unexpectedly stirred my heart. I'm ashamed to admit that talk of foreign missions used to bore me and I was afraid of the thought of it all. What they shared hit a deep chord with me. My life was still a mess at times, but God had brought me far in the healing process. I felt a strong desire to take the healing and comfort I'd received out into the world. Something came alive in me for the first time and I couldn't shake it.

Over time, the Lord brought more missionary friends into my life. Through these new friends I became familiar with Youth With a Mission (YWAM), a world-wide missions organization with training schools and outreach projects all over the world. Their central campus was located in Kona, Hawaii. I learned about a three-month classroom, lecture training that included a two-month outreach to third-world countries.

The specific training I was interested in was for people in my age range with children. My kids, then ages seven and thirteen, would attend a school designed for missionary kids where they continued their academics, but also received the missions training I would be getting on their level. The course was called, Crossroads Discipleship Training School. It prepared students who felt called to the mission field or Christian ministry, but needed training and experience.

The desire to go continually grew. I knew I had to make sure it wasn't just a personal desire of my own. My first reaction was that this is too far beyond reach and God couldn't be leading us down that road. It required money, which I didn't have. I also worried about what others would think. I told God if this was His idea, I needed Him to tell me, write it across the sky, or show me in the Bible, so I'd know for sure. I also told Him, as if He didn't know, that I didn't have any money and one way I'd know this was the path to take, was if a large sum of money fell into my lap. I felt this would settle the matter, as I doubted a large sum of money would just suddenly come in to my possession.

A few months passed and life got in the way, so I let this missions idea fall to the back burner to simmer. During quiet time one morning I continued reading where I'd left off in Jeremiah 6. I came to verse 16 and read, "This is what the Lord says: 'Stand at the crossroads and look; ask for the ancient paths, ask where the good way is, and walk in it, and you will find rest for your souls.' "

The words jumped off the page as I remembered the training school was called Crossroads and asked God if He was trying to get my attention again about this. The more I prayed about it, the more willing and excited I became. I felt this strongly in my heart, but reminded Him again of the money issue and that I was a single mom, as if He didn't already know this. I knew if it was God, He'd surely bring it up again, so I continued to wait.

During this time I was working part-time for a technical college in their single parent and displaced homemakers program called, "It's Your Turn". We assisted single parents and displaced homemakers who were returning to school or starting a new career. At work one day I was going through forms and filing papers when I read an article about a fairly new IRS credit for those who qualified called Earned Income Credit or EIC. I not only qualified for this credit, but had qualified for the past three years and never filed for it. I made a visit to my tax man and discovered I was due quite a large refund from the IRS. I immediately thought about buying a better car, clothes for the kids and saving the rest so I could breathe a little until I found the full-time job I'd been looking for.

Then my thoughts were boldly interrupted by a strong reminder of what I'd said to God about the large sum of money being the sign that He was leading us in this other direction. In my heart I knew it was God. I decided at that moment, I needed to take the first step and fill out the application for the Crossroads school, mail it and leave the next step in His hands.

My church family was very supportive and encouraging as I sought counsel and advice from close friends and leaders. The entire process took about a year and half from the first time I met the two young missionaries at our singles home group, until I made the decision to go. It was an exciting, scary and extremely faith-strengthening experience for me.

I had about six months to prepare. I learned that where God leads He will provide. I was able to pay for most of the tuition and set aside money for airfare. I bought passports, got shots and other necessities, which depleted the funds. There was a $1000 deposit required towards our room and board. It was due 30 days before our scheduled arrival and the deadline had arrived. As I was driving home from work the same day the money was due, I wondered why God brought me this far in the process only to seemingly shut the door. It was August 30, 1993, and I will never forget the drive home. I told God I was going to call the central office in Kona, Hawaii and tell them we weren't coming.

I picked up my daughter from the sitters, went home and searched for the phone number to call and cancel our registrations for the school and living quarters. Before I called, I noticed an envelope in the stack of mail I'd just picked up that looked like an IRS envelope. I thought I'd already received all that was due to me from them, and opened it expecting bad news. Instead it was a check for $1069!!! My daughter stared at me as I jumped up and down saying, "I did hear from God! It really was God! God, this really is You!" I called the office in Kona and told them a deposit was on the way and that we would see them in 30 days. All my doubt was gone, and I could focus on the continued preparations for this exciting adventure with the Lord.

Sometimes God will lead us into life-changing, uprooting decisions. This can be an exciting time because it requires all your trust and dependence on Him. You must completely abandon yourself and your life to His total care and provision. That particular time was without doubt one of the most thrilling experiences of my life, as He personally led me each step of the way.

The time spent at this school in Hawaii turned out to be the most blessed, fulfilling learning experience for us. I was so glad I took that leap of faith when I asked "Is this You, God?" The key with decisions like this is to pray and then wait. If this hadn't been God's leading, I believe He never would've continued growing the desire in my heart. If God is leading you to do something, He will open the doors as you seek Him, pray, read your Bible, seek godly counsel and wait.

I have one last story to share that completely reiterated to me Who my Husband truly was. Even though this was a wonderful time, I was still dealing with a controlling and manipulative ex-husband. Two weeks before we left for Hawaii, he married my best friend who he'd left me for. There was a time when I thought that would've killed me, but it didn't.

The irony of this last detail is that I was in beautiful Kona, Hawaii, learning more about this God I served and whom I'd begun to trust as my Husband. I was with 80 plus people from 11 different countries who were there for the same training. God met my children in wonderful ways and they were happy.

One day when we weren't in classes I ventured off alone to a nearby lagoon to swim. As I started the walk back to campus, the pristine beauty surrounding me was so captivating that I stopped to take some pictures. As I was digging in my bag for my camera, I had the strongest sense of Jesus' presence and suddenly felt like a bride on her honeymoon in Hawaii.

Only God could have worked out the timing of my ex-husband marrying my best friend and me being with Him in Hawaii. It was a powerful moment I'll never forget. There was no reason for the Lord to meet me in this way, other than He simply loves me and knows what I need, the same way He knows and loves each one who belongs to Him. I was very open to Him during this time and He had full access to my heart. This is just an example of what Jesus wants with you, if you open wide your heart and let Him in.

I've made a brief list below of the steps God may use in the leading process and what your part should be. When you're seeking His direction and praying about a big decision, allow these steps to unfold. You should never have to force anything to happen when God is doing the leading. He is an orderly God and will not mislead you.

God's Part

- God introduces a vision, idea or desire.

- He will support the desire/idea through His word, the Bible. He may also bring people in your path who support your vision.

- God will use circumstances in your daily life to consistently support your vision or idea.

- God will continue to use consistent circumstances and people around you.

- God will provide monetarily where He leads.

Your Part

- Pray and ask if this is from Him and read your Bible.

- Earnestly ask God to grow His desires in your heart and lessen the ones that aren't from Him. Seek godly counsel from friends and your pastor.

- Pay attention to any changing circumstances around you. If possible, take steps.

- Don't rush or try to force things, but take steps as He opens doors.

- Trust and surrender as you move forward in His plans.

It is vital in your relationship with the Lord, to stay close to Him, through daily quiet time, reading your Bible and sitting quietly with Him. Something I have to ask Him often is to keep my heart sensitive to his leading and make His desires become my desires. If I hadn't followed God's initial leading at this crossroads, I would've missed out on huge blessings and experiences I otherwise would have never known. Nothing is impossible when God is your central focus.

Are you at a crossroads right now? God may not be calling you to missions, to move to another state or change jobs. But if you desire to know Him deeper and hear Him speak to you, guess where that desire came from? He put that in your heart because He has so much to show you. God doesn't pick and choose certain people to speak to; He is looking for people who are simply available and whole-heartedly seeking Him.

Is there something holding you back from moving forward in the direction God may be leading you? Fear was a big obstacle for me. When I moved past the fear, there were other obstacles waiting for me. God dealt with the obstacles as I recklessly abandoned myself to Him.

You may be facing a decision or crossroads that isn't pressing or life altering. Do you feel God has placed an idea or desire in your heart, but you're not sure if it's really from Him?

There have been times I made a decision based on my emotions and desires that usually ended up in disaster. I'm not saying God never desires to give us our wants, but He won't do it if it's not His best for us. You don't give your kids everything they ask for because you know that everything they want isn't good for them.

God reveals His heart for us in Jeremiah 29:11-13, "For I know the plans I have for you, declares the Lord, plans to prosper you and not to harm you, plans to give you hope and a future. Then you will call upon me and come and pray to me, and I will listen to you. You will seek me and find me when you seek me with all your heart."

If God already knows the plans He's prepared for your life, don't you want to make sure you don't miss out on what He has for you? Seeking Him with all your heart doesn't mean just going to church on Sundays or praying when things get hard. It is a constant process in good times as well as bad times.

Call to Him, pray to Him, and seek Him with all your heart. When you do, your life will become full and exciting beyond what you could ever imagine!

"Stand at the crossroads and look, ask for the ancient paths; ask where the good way is and walk in it and you will find rest for your souls," Jeremiah 6:16 (NIV).

Marker Five: Reckless Abandonment

Have you ever done something careless and wild without giving any thought to what the consequences might be? I feel safe in saying that we all have at one time or another. What little fear you might have had was overridden by the thrill and excitement of what you were doing. When we were younger we were probably more daring and adventurous. As I've aged, my carefree adventures have lessened, mostly due to physical limitations, but also to a matured awareness of the consequences or possible dangers.

As a result of becoming more cautious, perhaps some of my opportunities have been missed. When I was a young girl, my summer days were spent in creeks, lakes and woods. Not once did I think about or see a poisonous snake, spider or wild animal, or get seriously hurt. I jumped in blankets of kudzu, swam out in the ocean, dragged my hands under rocks in creeks and swung from vines hanging from trees. What a great time I had! Just ten years ago I jumped out of a boat in the middle of the ocean with dive gear and descended 70 feet. Today I can't believe I even did that!

I still have an adventurous streak, but I'm safer with what I choose to do. A few years ago I zip-lined through trees in the North Carolina mountains, giving no thought of what would happen if the equipment didn't work properly. I trusted the guide when he told me it would hold 2000 pounds and their equipment had to be inspected and approved regularly. That's an activity I'd do again! Maybe.

For the most part I've become safe and boring. Most of it is due to severe hip arthritis and back pain, but I still worry about walking in the woods during the summer when all the critters are on the loose or swimming too far out in the ocean. These days I just consider my prudence as being wise, wouldn't you? There are just some things you don't do anymore when you grow up. I no longer abandon myself to such seemingly reckless adventures. However, regardless of any age, there is an exciting, daring adventure we can experience that has the best possible consequences with no dangers involved. While I was in my thirties I experienced this reckless adventure as a result of complete abandonment to Jesus Christ.

This particular period of my life was an incredible time with the Lord. I still walked through deep valleys and had to tread through the most difficult days, but I also experienced some of the most wonderful times as well. I let go of everything I kept trying to control. I walked in the joy of knowing that all my problems and battles belonged to Him. When I could have been pacing the floor at night, wringing my hands with worry, my mindset was that God was much more capable than I was in handling something I had no control over. At first, I felt guilty for not worrying about things, big things and little things. It seemed irresponsible and frivolous not to worry. But isn't that exactly the instruction we receive from God's Word?

This new reckless attitude is what led me into the adventure of my missions training in Hawaii and other missions experiences. Abandoning my life to God's care and provision was the most freeing and exciting thing I'd ever done. I had little fear of the unknown, trusting that God was in full control. My only job was to trust Him and handle only the things He set before me. The big problems were much easier to live through, with Him in charge, than if I'd tried to take care of them on my own.

The American Heritage Dictionary defines reckless as "heedless or careless; having no regard for consequences; adventurous, wild, audacious and daring." One of the definitions of abandon is "to yield oneself completely, as to emotion; a complete surrender of inhibitions; unbounded enthusiasm."

Living in reckless abandonment to Jesus brings about a sure and certain freedom that no man, job, amount of money, shiny new car or big house can bring. It causes a well of living water to rise up and quench all you thirst for. That's what the Samaritan woman discovered at the water well the day she met Jesus.

It was a typical, mundane day for her. Same-o-same-o, everyday stuff. Because she had been married five times and now lived with a man, I can't help but think she was a single mom. The Gospel of John doesn't record that she had children, but let's just use our imaginations. There was no birth control and she'd been with a lot of men. Unless she was unable to have children, there is a strong likelihood she was a mom.

In those days the community well was a place of gathering. In the cool of the morning, all the local women went to fill their jars with water for the day. I imagine they'd talk and socialize, catch up on the latest gossip. For some reason the Samaritan woman waited and went alone to the well at noon, the hottest part of day. Perhaps she was avoiding the other women because she had been shunned and considered a harlot. I believe Jesus purposely timed his rest stop; He knew when she would be coming to the well.

When she arrived at the well, Jesus was there waiting. When He asked her for a drink, she was stunned by the fact He even spoke to her because Jews didn't speak or socialize with Samaritans, especially women. She even stated this fact to Him and asked why He even asked her for water. Then Jesus replied, "If you knew the gift of God and who it is that asks you for a drink, you would have asked him and he would have given you living water" John 4:10. I can picture her face now as she realizes this isn't an ordinary man as He turns the conversation to God. She may even begin to feel a bit transparent, as though He can see into her heart and knows what she's thinking.

She replied, "Sir, you have nothing to draw with and the well is deep. Where can you get this living water" John 4:11? Jesus explains, "Everyone who drinks this water will be thirsty again, but whoever drinks the water I give him will never thirst. Indeed, the water I give him will become in him a spring of water welling up to eternal life" John 4:13-14. At this point, she didn't question or try to rationalize what He had said. She simply replied, "Sir, give me this water so that I won't get thirsty and have to keep coming here to draw water" John 4:15.

Then the conversation turned to the man she was living with and how Jesus knew she'd been married five times before. Their talk grew deeper as it turned to salvation and worshipping God in spirit and truth and that God was looking for true worshippers. She told Jesus that she knew Messiah was coming and He'd explain everything then. That's when Jesus revealed to her who He was.

When she realized Jesus was the true Messiah, she immediately dropped her water jar and ran to the nearest town to tell everyone she had just met Christ. Can you imagine her excitement? It sounds like she just left Jesus sitting there. Did He ever get the drink of water He'd asked her for? That's not even the point. He met her there, in the mundane of life, on purpose, with a motive to meet her need for His living water. That's what He wants to do for you.

This was a defining moment, a marker in her life. She abandoned herself to Him at the moment she dropped her water jar, and ran into town to tell everyone that she'd just met and talked with Jesus Christ. She wasn't concerned with shame and guilt anymore. She no longer cared what others thought. She let go of everything that held her back, and God used her because of her immediate trust and surrender. Because of her testimony, many of the Samaritans from the town believed in Him. Her life changed forever. She became a follower of Jesus and I'd be willing to guess she followed him all the way to Calvary.

So many of us can be like this women at the well. We go from man to man thinking he will take care of our needs and meet all our unrealistic expectations. We think this next man will satisfy our thirst much like this woman at the well. I love the way Jesus pursued her. He didn't condemn her. He rescued her. She didn't think twice about her reckless abandonment. She left her daily chores and immediately spread the news about Him. I would be willing to say she left the man she was living with to follow Jesus. Unless, of course, that man married her and they followed Jesus together. What can I say? I'm a hopeless romantic.

Do you know anyone like this woman? Could you be this woman? Do you sometimes feel like you live in a desert and need a drenching of His living water? All you have to do is respond to Him. I'm not talking about going to church or joining a small group or Bible study, volunteering or promising to spend more time reading your Bible. While these things should be a part of your life, they are to be the result of coming to the place of drinking and trusting fully in His pure, satisfying living water.

"For I have satiated the weary soul, and I have replenished every sorrowful soul" Jeremiah 31:25. Only Jesus can fully satisfy our souls. He alone has the power to reach in to the root of our hearts and water those areas that are thirsty and dry. The reason many of us don't fully surrender or abandon ourselves to Christ is because of fear and unbelief. Fear of what will be required once we do, and unbelief that He has the power to change us or our situation.

An even bigger reason is control. Our control. We cling to things we think we can control as if our life depended on it. Can you think of anything you truly have full control over? The truth is we don't have control over anything, except our choices and how we act. Sometimes we can't even control that. When we try to take things into our own hands and control them, it's like telling God that our way is better, and we'll use Him as a last resort, if necessary.

Do you want to live the spirit-filled life God has for you? God's promise for your future is hope and success, not to harm you. Fear of the unknown is why we choose what we're already comfortable with, even when it makes us bored and miserable. If we could just trust the unknowns to God, and go for it with Him, we would see more lives transformed and in return a changed world.

I allowed people and circumstances to persuade me to gradually drift from living a surrendered life. I have a huge regret to share with you. I hope it will help you if you are at a place in your walk with the Lord where you want to take that leap of faith, but you're thinking of all the reasons why you shouldn't. We can surrender portions of our lives to God or all of it. When I completely surrendered my life to Him during the time He was opening doors for my kids and I to attend the missions school in Kona, I had to let go of worrying what other people thought and do what I knew God was leading me to.

My family was somewhat supportive. About a month before we were due to leave, I was offered a full-time job where I currently worked part time. This was after God provided the $1000 deposit which confirmed for me that this was His leading. You can imagine my conversation with God when that job offer fell into my lap. When I asked God what was going on and what was He trying to show me, He gently spoke into my heart to ask them if they could hold the position for the time I would be gone. I planned to return and definitely wanted the job. I couldn't believe God was asking me to be so bold as to ask such a thing, but I did it anyway and they said, yes!

The regret I am referring to came towards the end of our three months in Hawaii. The three-month classroom training concluded with an optional two-month outreach, a hands-on experience with the class. Our class was scheduled to do our outreach phase in the Philippines and Indonesia. I desperately wanted to go. I was so torn between what others expected of me back home and my strong desire to go.

The three months I'd spent with these 80 people resulted in deep friendships, including several other single moms from Australia and California. Our kids became friends quickly and my children had also formed bonds with other missionary kids. When it came time to prepare for the outreach phase, I had another major decision to make. Many of my classmates, as well as the leaders of the school, strongly encouraged us to go. I was assured of God's provision and I have no doubt that if I'd made the decision to go on with the rest of the class, God would have provided. It would've deepened my trust even further, as well as my children's trust and belief in what God will do with available and surrendered lives.

I stood at this crossroads and did not ask God what I should do. The obstacles I faced became overwhelming. Instead, I allowed threats of a custody battle from my volatile, unpredictable ex-husband, the awaiting full-time job and pressure from family members to influence my decision. I made the easiest choice and decided to go home. It wasn't what I wanted to do, but fear set in and I told myself giving up the full-time job wasn't practical. I was doing what I thought everyone wanted me to do. Even though I felt as if I was leaving something prematurely, I convinced myself I really had no choice. It broke my heart.

We came home and I worked for two years with this technical college, commuting 40 miles one way and was miserable. I quit when I found a job closer to home for lesser pay. A year and a half passed, and ironically I was able to be rehired by the same technical college at a new campus they'd built closer to my home. I thought I'd made the right decision to leave the remainder of the training in

Hawaii. In hindsight, I believe God wanted us to stay and to walk in faith that He would provide for the out-reach phase.

This was in the Fall of '93, and I was rehired to work for the college at the new campus in the Summer of '97. It took me a long time to accept and admit that I'd made the wrong decision. I believe that I still would've been able to work for the school full time, just at a later time. I regret terribly allowing others to influence my decision. It turned out to be one of the most regrettable things I've ever done. Was God with me when I came home? Absolutely! Did He continue working powerfully in my life? No doubt about it. However, I do think I experienced repercussions of ending my missionary journey prematurely.

God did use what I'd learned in my training by allowing me to lead several short-term mission trips to Mexico and be part of a short-term missionary team in Honduras for two weeks. My missionary journey continues today in my home town, my job and my church. God has more than redeemed my mistake, as He has with many other mistakes I've made. I have to give Him my regrets so I don't waste time looking back. As I write this, I am in the midst of God bringing to reality a dream and vision I've had for single-parent ministry in my community. This is another story for another time.

I've thought about all the what-ifs and how different things might have been. It was hard not to think that I wasted what I learned in Hawaii, and that the years after coming home were a waste. But nothing is a waste with God and He has greatly used this in my life. I pray one of the ways may be right now with you, to let this be an example. Don't do as I did and give in to ungodly pressures and influence, when godly counsel and encouragement are leading you otherwise.

Is God bringing you to a place of reckless abandonment? If so, then let go and trust Him with the outcome. The main key in a surrendered and abandoned life to Jesus is staying in His word, praying and seeking godly counsel from friends and pastors who know you and are mature in the Lord. He will continually guide you in your journey as a single mom and turn all the chaos into order.

Living a life abandoned to Jesus doesn't mean He'll ask you to go to a foreign land or do something you don't want to do. He will fill your heart with the very desires of what He wants you to pursue. Then when your desires line up with His, He will fulfill them. It's a very exciting place to be. Will you drop your old, heavy water jar right where you are in full surrender and trust all the outcomes to Him? What will you lose by giving up your control to Him? Think about what you will gain.

"But whoever drinks the water I give him will never thirst. Indeed, the water I give him will become in him a spring of water welling up to eternal life" John 4:14.

Marker Six: God is Your Provider

There was a widowed single mom who had a young son. I don't know anything about their living conditions other than there was a drought and famine where they lived. She'd gone out to gather a few sticks for a fire so she could bake their last meal using the handful of flour and few drops of oil she had left. In her mind, they were going to eat their last meal and then die of starvation. I imagine she worried that she might die first, leaving her son with no mother to comfort him as he starved to death.

While she was gathering the sticks, a stranger came into town. He approached her asking for a drink of water and a cake of bread, explaining he was tired and hungry from his journey. She explained to him that all she had was a handful of flour and small bit of oil. He told her not to be afraid, but to go back to her house and bake a small cake for him first, then another for her and her son. He assured her that God would not let the bin of flour be used up and the jar of oil run dry.

She believed he was a man of God and didn't question what he told her to do. I'm sure she'd heard of Elijah's predictions of the drought and famine and believed he was a godly prophet. I try to imagine what must have gone through her mind as she prepared this bread for him. Maybe Elijah's unusual request gave her a glimmer of hope, as she thought about his promise of not running out of flour and oil. She knew enough about God to know He was a God of miracles and hoped for a miracle for her and her son.

Her trust and obedience led to a miraculous provision. "For the jar of flour was not used up and the jug of oil did not run dry, in keeping with the word of the Lord spoken by Elijah" I Kings 17:16. In other words, God kept His word. This single mom never ran out of food and they lived through the famine. It amazes me that out of all the people in this town of Zarephath, God chose to use a poor, discouraged single mom to provide for this godly prophet. Then through her obedience, God provided indefinitely for her and her son.

Has God given you a promise about something? Have you trusted and obeyed Him in the things He's given you to do? Has He done something miraculous in your life that caused your faith to soar and your doubts to take flight? There are many promises from His word that I held onto throughout my single-parent years. Some have been fulfilled, but there are some I'm still believing and waiting to come to fulfillment.

Have I always trusted and obeyed God in everything He's told me to do? Sadly, I haven't. I've had many times of struggling, doubting and being frustrated with His timing. The bottom line is I am fully persuaded that God says what He means and means what He says. If He's given me hope about a situation through His Word and the assurance He always fulfills His promises, then that settles it for me. The timing and circumstances are up to Him and not on my timetable.

Things haven't always worked out like I thought they should or wanted. When life doesn't happen the way we think would be best, trusting that God has a better plan is the key to peace. If you're constantly trying to push open a door, maybe God is on the other side causing the resistance to protect you from something. He continually reminds me that it's better to depend on Him to lead me to the door and let Him open it. After all, He is the Gentleman. Then I can confidently walk through the open door, knowing that He's doing the leading.

The widowed, single mom's faith must have soared and grown stronger after this huge miracle in her life. Then she faces a terrible crisis. Her little boy gets seriously sick. Her unwavering faith must have weakened as his condition worsened. I imagine her faith shattered while she took care of him only to see him get worse and then die. I think she must have been confused and angry with God, after He'd miraculously provided during the famine only to allow her son to get sick and die.

She then questioned her own existence. In 1 Kings 17:18, we get a glimpse of her emotional and spiritual state as she confronts Elijah. "What have I to do with you, O man of God? Have you come to me to bring my sin to remembrance, and to kill my son" (NJK)? It sounds as though her past sins, whatever they were, came back to haunt her as she walked through yet another potentially faith-shattering experience. Isn't that just like us? Sometimes when we face hard times, we think God is punishing us for a past sin. God blows that concept out of the water for her by what He does next.

Elijah told her to give him her son. She handed her son over to him, and Elijah took him out of her arms, carried him to the room where he was staying and laid him on his bed. "Then he cried out to the Lord and said, 'O Lord my God, have you also brought tragedy on the widow with whom I lodge, by killing her son?' Then he stretched himself out on the child three times, and cried out to the Lord and said, 'O Lord my God, I pray, let this child's soul come back to him' " I Kings 17:20 (NKJ).

It seems that even Elijah struggled with God as he was extremely distraught over the boy's death. Regardless of the bleak circumstances, Elijah still believed and trusted God as he persisted in prayer, refusing to give up. He turned to the Lord, cried out in distress and passion. I imagine Elijah had grown close to the little boy during the time he lived in the widow's home, possibly developing a type of father-son relationship.

Continuing in Verses 22-24, we discover, "The Lord heard the voice of Elijah and the soul of the child came back to him and he revived. And Elijah took the child and brought him down from the room back into the house, and gave him to his mother. And Elijah said, 'See, your son lives!' Then the woman said to Elijah, 'Now by this I know that you are a man of God, and that the word of the Lord in your mouth is the truth' " (NKJ).

God's compassion for this single mom is evident. He is fully aware of the very difficult job all single parents face. Sometimes it seems impossible to focus on God's promises and trust Him, rather than the immediate problem you are facing. When Elijah showed up on the scene and asked for water and bread from this woman, it seemed he would have been a burden to her. Instead he turned out to be a huge blessing and tool through which God provided for this woman and her son. God's provisions can come through the most unlikely sources.

Have you ever felt like this mother? She came out of a crisis due to God's provision, including a new godly friend, only to be thrust into another crisis when her son got sick and died. For years it seemed I would come through a crisis, only to find myself in the middle of another one. As I look back, God was with me in all of them. He either walked me through the trial until it ended, or simply snatched me out of it. Either way it was always by His strong arm that I could carry on.

Sometimes I experienced tough times due to my own choices and had to endure the consequences. I would blame God or feel He'd abandoned me. Those are the times I had to admit I'd gone ahead of Him and made a decision based on what I wanted before truthfully asking Him and waiting for Him to lead.

I remember a time when I was struggling financially and couldn't afford groceries. Our cupboards were almost empty. I didn't always have child support and I didn't make that much money from my job to support three people. I remember being at a very low point and trying to be strong for the kids. Sometimes I would share our needs with someone I trusted and other times I wouldn't tell anyone when we had a need. I got tired of always being the one in need and struggled with pride and asking for help. So, I would take it straight to God, looking to Him to provide, which is what I'd done this particular time.

During this time, I asked my son to watch his little sister so I could take a bath. While I was in the bathroom, he went to get something out of our car. Then he came to the bathroom door and asked me why I'd left boxes of groceries in the backseat of the car. I had no clue what he was talking about because I hadn't bought any groceries. He talked to me through the door telling me there were boxes of food in the backseat of the car. I immediately knew God had provided somehow.

Can you imagine how I felt as I went to the car and my son and I carried in box after box of food? I wondered the whole time how anyone even knew how bad our need was. The only thing that mattered was God knew. It didn't matter how the food got there. I just knew it was one of those unexplained provisions. That day my faith was strengthened and I soared. Every time I faced a crisis and trusted God to the fullest of my ability, He would come through, and my faith would get stronger each time.

The widowed mom must have felt that way when she thought she and her son were going to die, then God provided in the most unexpected way. Her faith was strengthened and she felt cared for by God. "He provides food for those who fear Him. He remembers his covenant forever" Psalm 111:5.

When I say God is our provider, I'm not only talking about money, food and shelter, which He does provide. He also provides direction and stability for anyone seeking Him and trusting Him to meet all their needs. Our needs are far too many to expect them to be met by this world or other people. God does use people and circumstances, but the important thing here is that you don't put your hope and trust in His provision, but in Him alone.

I don't want to give you the impression that I always held my head high and trusted Him without all the fretting we women can do. I often struggled. In those times I would turn to Him and His Word for strength. I would read, "Rest in the Lord, and wait patiently for Him...Do not fret, it only causes harm" Psalm 37:7-8 (NKJ). I knew all I needed to do was to place my trust in Him and He would take care of us. That didn't mean I sat around and did nothing. I was to handle the tasks He placed in front of me, including the job He provided, and trust Him to handle our needs. It was not easy, but trusting Him has proven to be much more profitable than wringing my hands with worry and fret.

The Webster's New College Dictionary defines fret as "to wear away by gnawing, rubbing, corroding and to become eaten, worn and frayed." This is a vivid description of someone who worries and frets over everything. Women can be the best worriers and fretters I've ever seen. Somehow we feel that if we're not worrying, then we're not good mothers and fulfilling the true calling of motherhood.

There were many times when I felt God didn't hear my prayers at all. Then there were times when I felt He not only heard my cry, but answered far beyond my wildest expectations. Sometimes He provided before I even asked. Sometimes I would ask and have to wait. I used say to the Lord, "why is it that You seem to work in my life in the 11ᵗʰ hour and 59ᵗʰ second?"

Sometimes I had real physical needs like food and electricity. I couldn't sit back and just wait for Him. But when I'd pray before making that necessary phone call to the electric company He'd go before me and make provision. Or when I'd pray as I'm walking into the grocery store with my last $10, He'd show me the best way to spend it so that we had enough food. I didn't always handle these things this way, but when I did it always turned out for the best.

I know it's hard not to compare your life with others. At times I struggled with not resenting having to depend on God for every single thing. All I wanted was to just be able to wake up each morning and not worry about money or needs that couldn't be ignored for one more day. But those were the very things God used to build my faith and trust in Him.

A persistent faith flowing out of a mother's heart is irresistible to the Lord. Sometimes I would imagine my faint, feeble cry barely reaching His ears. Then other times I'd imagine my bold, confident request shooting straight through the dark universe, surpassing all the stars and reaching loudly to His ears. The truth is your voice only has to travel as far as your next breath because He is always right there with you, saying to you, "Fear not, I will help you" Isaiah 41:13 (NKJ).

Today the financial struggles are not as severe, but I sometimes miss those desperate times with the Lord where I relied solely on Him. The truth is there is always a need I have that even my husband or best of friends can never provide. God will always be my provider in all things, no matter what my needs are.

You may not have the same kinds of financial struggles I did. You may struggle with other areas where you feel God has deprived you or hasn't provided what you feel you need or deserve. He wants to be your Provider in every aspect of your life. The key is to trust His timing, and know without a doubt that He sees the bigger picture. There are times when I don't understand, but I know I'm not called to understand. I'm called to trust Him.

I don't know what situation or need you're facing today. He does. Take all your needs to Him. He knows what they are even "before you ask" Matthew 6:8.

"And my God shall supply all your need according to His riches in glory by Christ Jesus" Philippians 4:19 (NKJ). My prayer is that you will take full advantage of all He has provided. One of my favorite verses in scripture reminds me how He desires to meet all our needs through His grace and mercy. "Let us therefore come boldly to the throne of grace that we may obtain mercy and find grace to help in time of need" Hebrews 4:16 (NKJ).

Go boldly before Him. He's there waiting for you.

"For thus says the Lord God of Israel: 'The bin of flour shall not be used up, nor shall the jar of oil run dry, until the day the Lord sends rain on the earth' " I Kings 17:14 (NKJ).

Marker Seven: Tamasa

It was an extremely hot summer in Conyers, Georgia, in July of 1999. My daughter and I lived in what I called a rented "cracker-jack box" house that didn't have central air. My son, by this time, was 18 and living with his dad. (Another story for another time) We had two window air conditioner units that I turned on, only when we were home because I didn't want to run up the electric bill. I was tired, depressed and at an all-time low. I was recovering from a break up with the only boyfriend I'd had since my divorce. Feeling sorry for myself and wallowing in self-pity was keeping me very busy. For the first time in my sixteen-year walk with the Lord I struggled with thoughts of throwing in the towel. I still went to church and stayed involved, but was simply going through the motions. I was ready to quit.

Throughout the years prior, it had been my unmoving faith in the Lord that had gotten me through my divorce and the hardships that followed. Now I was wavering, something I never thought would happen to me. I knew enough of God to know I had no choice but to hang on and keep trusting in Him. I desperately hoped for that light at the end of the tunnel. I was at a breaking point, and in my mind, relief needed to come soon or I was going to crack.

During this time, a group from my church was preparing for a two-week mission trip to Honduras. They would be working alongside an international mission organization, to help rebuild a

Honduran village affected by the deadly floods caused by Hurricane Mitch in the Fall of 1998. I never considered going because it was a construction trip that I felt was a job for men and I didn't have any money to put into a trip like this. Besides, I was feeling too sorry for myself to even think about trying to help someone else. What could I possibly have to offer anyone in Honduras?

As I dropped my daughter off at school one morning, the car in front of me had a bumper sticker that read, "I Love Honduras". This was very odd in a small, Metro Atlanta suburb all those years ago. I took it as a hint to pray for our team that was preparing to go. Then again that same week, when I dropped my daughter off at school, a different car had a similar sticker on it that said something about Honduras. These bumper stickers no longer seemed coincidental, so I asked God, "Lord, are you telling me I should think and pray about going?" I said a simple prayer, along with reminding Him I didn't have the money, I'd have to get a passport, shots, and put in for vacation time, etc., etc.

That following Sunday at church I was handed a white envelope from an anonymous donor with cash inside. I don't remember how much it was, but it was enough of an answer for me. I explained to the leader of the Honduran mission team what had been going on, and she encouraged me to start making plans to go. The team was a mix of men and women, so I didn't feel too out of place. My other best friend Susan, who God had placed in my life was also going.

I was more nervous than excited about going on this type of trip because the conditions were going to be rough. I doubted if I was doing the right thing by going, but couldn't shake the feeling that this was the Lord's leading. My job approved the time off. My daughter would be on summer break and could stay with her dad for the days I would be gone. My passport came in quicker than expected. Our team was prepared with the required vaccines, malaria pills and mosquito netting. I also remember thinking the hot house I was living in was good preparation for the heat in Honduras.

When the day came to leave for Honduras and temporarily put my painful existence on hold, my excitement grew. I was ready to go far away, get my hands dirty and focus on something other than my problems. I would also be with close friends from my church and looked forward to this God adventure. All the preparations we'd done before leaving could not have prepared me for what I would learn on this trip from another single mom, which would change my life forever.

We arrived in Monjaras on a big yellow school bus. Dozens of kids from the little village ran to the bus to greet us with hugs and smiles. This is where we'd stay for the next ten days. This particular village had been devastated by the ravaging floods, and some of the villagers had pieced together homes from sticks, corrugated metal and heavy plastic, all held together with dried mud.

We were combined with another group from California and assigned to three families to help rebuild their homes. Our temporary residence was called the "community center" by all the villagers. I called it the Compound. It was made of gray cinder block walls, topped with chicken wire where air could flow through. The first thing I saw upon entering the building was a small sign hanging from the ceiling that read, "Welcome to Club Med."

There was a section in the back for sleeping, one side for males, the other for females. There were green army cots for each of us where we unrolled our sleeping bags and hung mosquito netting. There were about eleven women and only five fans to cool us off at night while we slept. We crowned one of our team members, Maureen (Mo), the fan queen, as she strategically engineered all the fans in such a way that everyone had air blowing on them at night.

The front part of the building had a makeshift kitchen and an area blocked off for "bowl baths". There was an area across from the kitchen that held the machinery for sawing wood, cutting rebar and making cinder blocks. The outhouse was, well…outside. Even in these conditions, it didn't take long to settle into a routine, and get to know the kids and some of the local residents from the village.

We had been in Monjaras for several days when I was scheduled to go to a different work site with other team members who had already been there. At first I was a little upset because I'd already started getting to know the family we were working with and now I'd been redirected. I was sure it wasn't because my great labor skills were needed, but soon learned it was because of a work God needed to do in me.

On the way to the site, I asked my teammates questions about the new family. I was told it was a young woman with three kids. I was also told she had the cleanest outhouse in the village and if you had to "go", you could feel safe using her outhouse. I asked what family members were going to work with us. As part of the requirements for a new house, there had to be two family members to work with us in the construction of their new home.

When I asked about the father, the story was that he'd left them a while back, walked away never to return. The mom and her fourteen-year old son were going to work with us. Her other two children were too young. I was instantly intrigued. Sitting in the back of the flatbed truck, as we bumped along the dirt road to her house, I thought to myself, "*A single mom. How does a woman with three young kids survive out here with hurricanes, floods, 110 degree temperatures and the constant threat of diseases?*" I pictured a small, frail woman with a tired and sad face.

We arrived in the old flat-bed truck in front of her makeshift house of sticks, mud and leftover plastic. Her roof consisted of whatever clay tiles she salvaged from the flooding. I jumped off the back of the truck and observed the house. Pieces of plywood were "weaved" through the gaps between the sticks for privacy, as the front of her house faced the dirt road. There was no door to close, just a walkway. We started unloading the supplies off the truck and were instructed to slide the two-by-fours through the gaps in the house.

I carried some of the wood into her house and that's when I saw her. Tamasa was sweeping the dirt floor of her mud and stick house and tidying up as we started unloading the wood into her "living room." She greeted us with a beautiful smile showing us where to store the lumber we were sliding through the gaping holes of her one-room house. We would use the lumber later for the roof. The environment was a busy one with everyone already hard at work. I wonder if I looked like a wide-eyed kid trying to take in my surroundings. I tried to keep from staring at Tamasa as I felt an immediate connection to her.

I stood inside her house gazing at the interior walls of dried mud and sticks. Large pieces of plastic covered one side of the house, which I later learned was the direction the wind and rain blew during rainstorms. The hammocks they slept in hung from the ceiling to one side of the room. Even though it was dark inside, sunlight streamed through from another door-less walkway that led to the back side of her house. I walked through and stepped outside the back. That's when I saw the famous outhouse tucked back into the lush greenery that made up her backyard. Her efficient, tidy clothes-washing system was set up outside.

I met her oldest son, thin, handsome and already working, with his work gloves and shovel in hand. Her daughter followed her mom closely as if not wanting to let her out of her sight, and the youngest boy was all over the place with unhindered excitement.

I was struck by Tamasa's beauty. Her big, dark eyes and hair complimented her creamy, brown skin. She didn't look at all like I had imagined, hopeless, tired and depressed, like me. She was young, pretty, very hospitable and obviously excited to see us. I was overwhelmed by their living conditions, yet extremely humbled by the tidiness of her home and gracious hospitality.

For days we worked side by side in 100+ temperatures and high humidity. Every afternoon, she would leave the site and walk into the nearest town. Since she spoke no English and my Spanish was more like chopped Spanglish, I had to ask other people questions about her so I could find out more about her. I learned she had a part-time job which she walked to every afternoon, leaving her fourteen-year old son to care for the two younger siblings.

As I spent more time with Tamasa on the work site, I became aware of changes happening in me. I thought about my own home back in Georgia and how I thought I had it so bad. My house didn't have central air, but I did have two window air conditioners. I had windows and doors I could lock at night or close during heavy rain storms. My house had a bathroom with clean running water and a flushing toilet. My floors weren't made of dirt, but were all covered with carpet. I felt ashamed as I watched her sweep her floors every day and clean the outhouse, mix cement, layer concrete blocks with us, then walk into town to her job.

One day I asked Tamasa if I could take a picture of her family to remember them by. She didn't respond with yes or no, but walked away from me calling her three kids to come inside the house. I thought I'd offended her or maybe my broken Spanish wasn't clear. After what seemed like an hour, Tamasa and her children emerged from their house dressed in their finest clothes and their hair fixed to pose for my picture. A rush of emotions escaped me with tears of humility as we searched for the perfect place they could stand for their family portrait.

While taking their picture I was flooded with a surge of emotion, knowing our time together would soon end and I'd never see her again. I hugged her neck telling her how much God loved her. I wanted to convey how valued and loved she was by God. I wanted her to know God had a plan for her life. She just smiled and nodded. Something told me she understood and believed and trusted in the Lord. In my attempt to encourage her, I realized she was the one encouraging me, not with words, but by her countenance and the way she lived her life.

God didn't send me on this mission trip because he needed me there to do a job. He could have accomplished it all without my help. I was broken, burned out and wavering in my relationship with Him. He needed me to go so He could open my eyes and do a permanent work in my life. He used another single mom who had nothing materially to accomplish this.

Tamasa endured a hurricane and devastating floods that washed away her home and all she possessed. She was abandoned by her husband, and left to take care of three children alone in unspeakable conditions. She didn't have the resources that I had back home in Georgia and faced diseases and sicknesses that were a constant threat in her area. She took pride in her makeshift home, sweeping dirt floors every day and making sure her outhouse was spotless and her children cared for.

Our last day came all too soon. Our team boarded the yellow school bus that would take us away from the village to the capitol city, Tegucigalpa, eventually to the airport and then home. I sat on the bus looking out the window at all the village children along with a few adults who had come to see us off, waving, hugging team members goodbye and crying.

I looked into the sea of faces and there stood Tamasa with her kids, waving and smiling. The calm, peaceful smile I had come to know broke my heart as she stood there strong and confident. I didn't want to leave. Something in me had changed though. I felt renewed and thankful. I was ready to get back to my life at home and tackle the challenges I left behind just two weeks prior. I had a changed heart and renewed hope that only God can give.

When I came home and walked through the front door of my rented "cracker-jack box" house, I felt incredibly rich. I was overwhelmed with the material possessions God had blessed me with. A refrigerator to keep food in, beds to sleep in and carpeted floors. The walls were freshly painted and my car was parked in the one-car garage. It was stifling hot inside my house, so I simply walked over to the window air conditioner and flipped on the switch. I noticed I had electricity, lights and clean, running water. My list just kept growing.

I suddenly saw all the things I did have and not what I didn't have. Having a thankful heart was going to keep me busier than feeling sorry for myself ever did. What I didn't have didn't matter anymore. And more than the material blessings God for some reason chose to give me, I had Him, just like Tamasa, and no one can take that away. She knew God was her provider. She and her children had survived Hurricane Mitch and the floods. She survived her husband leaving. And because she didn't give up hope, she now had a brand new home in Monjaras, Honduras, to live in and raise her children. If Tamasa could be a survivor, I too would survive.

The years following the mission trip brought more hardships and disappointments. When I thought I was being deprived of material things I felt God should give me, I'd remember Tamasa and her life in Honduras. My perspective would quickly change and my selfish, needy prayers became prayers of thanksgiving and praise for God's grace and provision for all I had materially and spiritually. God used Tamasa to place this huge marker in my life.

Being thankful for God's many blessings reaches far beyond our material possessions that come with price tags. This is often ignored in our materialistic society. Tamasa knew what really mattered. She had to know. Her obvious faith proved this. I'll never forget her and all I learned from her simple, yet profound life.

"Thanks be to God for His indescribable gift," II Corinthians *9:15 (NKJ)!*

Marker Eight: Waiting

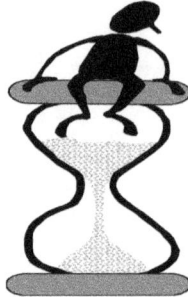

Do you feel like you're always waiting for something? Whether you're waiting in line, in traffic, in a doctor's office or for Mr. Right to come sweep you off your feet, waiting isn't pleasant. I haven't met anyone yet who enjoys it. In America we've become conditioned to always be in a hurry. The drive-thru window is as common as sliced bread. We have drive-through restaurants, banks and coffee shops. There are drive-through dry cleaners and drug stores. I've even seen a place where you can drive up to a window, order some groceries and Voila, you have groceries! While these conveniences are a need for the elderly and handicapped, I wonder if it hasn't caused the rest of us to become lazy and impatient.

Everything is instant. We have instant foods, instant messaging and instant internet. Waiting for something has become a thing of the past as we rush into the future with all our electronic communicating devices and fast, immediate services of all kinds. Somehow we've become a society where we think we deserve to have what we want right now and shouldn't have to wait for it.

We can become nasty and rude if we have to stand in line for any length of time, even if we have nowhere else to be. We're unkind to the waitress who has other tables to wait on. We hate being put on hold on the phone. Generally, we have become a very impatient bunch of human beings. The more I think about it, the more shameful it is.

Right now you might be waiting for that godly husband, a raise at work or that dream house you've always wanted. There are some amazing promises from the Lord Jesus for those who wait for Him to bring about those things they need and want. He doesn't promise it's easy. The promises for those who are willing to wait bring the deepest joy and contentment beyond anything the world could ever deliver. The world fails on its promises, bringing frustration and disappointment. But the Lord won't. He always keeps His promises. We see the evidence all throughout the Bible and in our personal lives today when we walk closely with Him.

It seems that waiting has been the running theme of my life. Waiting for long periods of time to be able to buy certain things or take a vacation was the norm for me. I'm still waiting for God to answer certain deep and personal prayers. I've waited to see God bring justice in numerous situations. When I tell people I was single for nineteen years, waiting until God brought the right man, they have a hard time believing that. I also had to be in the right place spiritually to even recognize who that guy was for me. What about you? Are you waiting for God to answer specific prayers? Maybe you're waiting for God to restore a torn relationship, release you into ministry or open doors for a new career.

It's what we do while we're waiting that's most important. Sometimes we can take things into our own hands and try to bring about what we're waiting for so we don't have to wait anymore. Remember Sarah when she got tired of waiting for God to bless her with a child? She took matters into her own hands and told her husband to sleep with Hagar, her servant. If you want to know and experience God's direction for your life, then waiting on Him is essential. If we take matters into our own hands, then we have to be prepared to reap the consequences. If we're not willing to wait on God's timing, we can be sure we'll miss out on God's better plan for our life and always have to wonder, what if.

I've been reluctant to share this next story because I'm not proud of what I did when I wanted something so badly. I moved forward, even when I felt God's restraint. For years all I could afford to live in was a small rental house or apartment. I was sick of paying rent and wanted a home of my own. I had a steady full-time job, as well as an additional part-time job on weekends. I'd finally gotten to the place where I could qualify for a house.

I prayed and even felt encouraged by a scripture in Psalm 113:7-9, "He raises the poor out of the dust, and lifts the needy out of the ash heap, that He may seat him with princes. With the princes of His people He grants the barren woman a home, like a joyful mother of children" (NKJ). I was so sure this was God's promise that He was going to make it possible for me to buy my own house. I still believe those verses, but I thought they meant my waiting was over.

I didn't shop around very long. I felt rushed by other circumstances such as my daughter having to change schools and working out car pools, etc. I found a small house right across the street from some good friends I'd known for years, so they could even vouch for the neighborhood. The man I was currently renting a house from even let me use a month's rent as a down payment and be a little late paying my rent that month. I also qualified for a first-time buyer loan and even had a friend who inspected the house at no charge.

Everything seemed to be right in line with God's leading, until my loan officer kept requesting more documentation, and proof of debts I'd paid off and current utility bills. She assured me I was still going to get the loan, but they just needed more documentation. It just prolonged my waiting. The process was becoming more difficult for the loan to be approved. The joy and excitement of home buying was turning into an aggravation.

The friend who'd inspected the house, had concerns about some major issues and potential problems. One of my best friends, Susan, was leery of the house and encouraged me to keep looking. I remember thinking if it was this difficult it might not be the best thing, but I wanted it more than being willing to pay attention to the red flags. I continued to force the process, never questioning God along the way if this particular house was the right one for us.

My loan was finally approved and a closing date set. In the meantime I'd been preparing for a mission trip to Mexico and was leaving the day after my house closing. I felt rushed and I didn't have time to keep looking. School was beginning soon after our return from Mexico, and we needed a permanent address in order to register my daughter to attend. It would be her junior year of high school and I felt it was important for her to start in this particular school district and be able to finish there.

There were other issues surrounding my timeline, but the biggest mistake I made was not wholeheartedly consulting God and taking my wise friends' advice. The whole house-buying effort had become all about me and what I wanted, while I excluded God from this undertaking. I also allowed this hectic time of my life to distract me from what was really important. I could have stopped the entire process, waited, shopped around some more and taken more time, rather than rushing ahead of what had potential to become a huge blessing. Instead it ended up being a big, bad mistake.

I went to the closing prepared for a specific house payment and terms of the loan. I was ignorant of some hidden costs and for reasons I can't recall, my loan had slightly changed. My monthly mortgage payments were going to be a bit more than I'd planned, with a five-year variable changing rate rather than fixed. Somehow I was getting a large check at the end of closing.

At the closing table with the attorneys, real estate agent and loan officer sitting around the big oval conference table, I looked over the papers as they explained the terms of the loan and why I was getting a check at closing. I felt a strong tug on my heart and a restraint that I felt was from God, but I ignored it. I convinced myself that God was in this and everything was going to be fine. How could I back out now? I had to hurry home and pack for the mission trip to Mexico. I thought to myself, "God promised me, so everything will be fine." And everything was…..for a while.

I signed all the papers, shook their hands and even felt "taken" as I saw the satisfied smile on the loan officer's face as I left her office. I didn't feel like I could stop the process and refuse to go through with the purchase. I would've been too embarrassed. I didn't think I could take more time to continue house hunting, and so much had already transpired by this point. I just held onto God's promise about having my own home. That was indeed His promise, but I now know not that house, not that type of loan, not that time.

I owned that house for two and a half years before losing it to foreclosure. About a month after the closing, that loan company sold my mortgage to another company, so I understood why they took the risk with me. I started noticing major problems with the house. After living there about a year, I hurt my back at my other part-time job and could no longer hold that job.

My daughter's senior year brought more expenses than I was prepared for. Her father went to prison and what little child support I was getting ended. I could no longer afford my mortgage, which increased after the first and second year with the variable loan I had.

I struggled financially and entered a crisis with my faith, as I continued to believe God had led me in this direction. I tried to do a short sell and found someone who made an offer, but the mortgage company denied it, even after I wrote a hardship letter. I'd already moved out and found myself in the renting world again.

I questioned God as my faith grew weak. I doubted my ability to hear from Him anymore. I couldn't understand why this was happening. Then He gently reminded me of the closing day and how I felt His restraint before signing the papers. I ignored His warning from my friends and the warning from the Holy Spirit as I signed the papers.

I found mercy and grace with God as I repented and took responsibility for what happened. I still had to deal with the consequences of ruining my credit, and carrying the shame and guilt of losing my house. If I'd just waited a little longer and prayed about every step of house hunting and educated myself in the loan process, I am confident my home-buying experience would have a completely different result with a much better outcome.

Is there something you're waiting for and you feel you've waited long enough? Whatever it is, it is worth waiting for God's timing and provision. "I waited patiently for the Lord, He turned to me and heard my cry" Psalm 40:1.

If you're waiting to see justice, read Psalm 25:9, "The humble He guides in justice" (NKJ). Make sure your heart is humbled.

When you're feeling weak and weary, read Psalm 27:13-14. "I would have lost heart, unless I had believed that I would see the goodness of the Lord in the land of the living. Wait on the Lord, be of good courage, and He shall strengthen your heart. Wait, I say, on the Lord" (NKJ)!

Trust God's timing and trust that He has your best interest at heart. Please, please, please don't learn the hard way like I did.

Never ignore His restraint in a situation no matter how badly you want something. "The word of the Lord is proven, He is a shield to all who trust in Him" Psalm 18:30 (NKJ). He couldn't shield me from the disaster I brought on myself because I'd stepped ahead of Him, shoving aside His warnings.

He longs to give us good things and only blessings will follow your wait. We read in Isaiah 30:18, "Yet the Lord longs to be gracious to you. He rises to show you compassion. For the Lord is a God of justice. Blessed are all who wait for him!" Forging ahead without seeking God's direction, will bring difficult consequences later. Will you choose His blessings by waiting?

"But those who wait on the Lord, shall renew their strength, they shall mount up with wings like eagles, they shall run and not be weary, they shall walk and not faint," Isaiah 40:31 (NKJ).

Marker Nine: Victim or Victor?

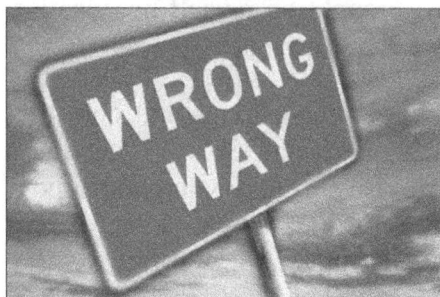

Have you ever been a victim? I don't think anyone's answer to that question would be no. Maybe you've been a victim of gossip, slander or betrayal. Maybe you've been a victim of sexual, physical or mental abuse. We've all been victims to varying degrees. Oftentimes, without realizing it, our victimization causes us to react to life events in dysfunctional ways.

If you've been betrayed by someone you loved, it hinders your ability to trust. We can go through life reacting to people and circumstances out of our experiences as victims.

I want to clarify something before I go any further. After years of allowing myself to be held as a victim by my ex-husband, the Lord graciously enabled me to forgive him. That didn't excuse the harm done. There was a time I deeply wanted him to suffer, but today I am sad he chooses to live a life apart from God. I do hope and pray that one day he will enjoy the benefits and blessings of a surrendered life to Christ. My ex-husband is not my enemy. As a believer in Christ, our true enemy is satan and that is who we battle.

I was a victim of betrayal of the deepest kind. My husband secretly pursued an affair with a woman who called me her best friend, so I felt doubly betrayed. I was also a victim of mental and emotional abuse of great magnitudes. A couple of years following our divorce, I finally took a stand and attempted to set boundaries, making it clear he couldn't cross certain lines. This is when he began to exhibit behavior I'd never seen before. He became threatening, volatile and extremely verbally abusive. I'd never dealt with this type of unpredictable behavior. I didn't know who he was anymore.

I worked very hard during the years following our divorce to keep the peace where the kids were concerned, but it was difficult. I became afraid of him and knew what buttons not to push. I reacted to life out of the experiences surrounding our relationship. I'd healed from the heartbreak, but still allowed fear to control me. The affect he had over me was sickening. I couldn't be friends with men, even strong Christian men. I became cynical and critical about all men.

Outwardly I would put men down, but secretly longed for a relationship with a godly man. I built a protective wall around me sending out signals that I was unapproachable. I somehow thought I deserved the abuse. I felt unworthy and unlovable, believing men would never find me interesting or desirable. When I would talk about my problems with someone, I always referred to what had been done to me and wanted people to pity me. I was a victim.

Because of my experience, I developed a growing burden for abused women. One day I was talking with my pastor, Mark, about why women leave their abusive relationships only to go back to their abuser. Mark stated that they live in a victim mentality and don't see a way out. He further explained that someone with a victim mentality thinks they deserve the abuse and somehow they're to blame. They feel inferior and unworthy, and continue to allow that person control over them. This type of living becomes so familiar it feels normal.

The more he described this woman, the more I realized I was her. Thankfully, it was after my husband left me that he became so abusive, so I never lived in physical abuse. Even though I had victory over the betrayal and heartache, I still allowed his fearful manipulations to control me. His verbal attacks and threats tore away at my identity as a woman and mother. I found myself believing the lies, which were the exact opposite of what God said about me.

When I was with friends, family or at church events, I was happy, fulfilled and confident. Whenever I had to face him about an issue with the kids or money, I became another person. I shrunk inside, felt sick and weak, allowing him control over everything out of fear. If I said no or wouldn't agree with him about an issue, I suffered intensely. I thought I had no choice but to endure this and that it would never change.

After realizing I acted and thought like a victim, but didn't have to, I began changing how I responded to him. If a phone conversation became abusive, I ended it by hanging up. If he threatened me in any way, I was prepared to take lawful actions. I realized that most of his threats held no weight, but were just manipulative tactics to control me. The biggest change was praying boldly and confidently ahead of time when I knew I would have to deal with him. I searched my Bible for answers about this and found much on the subject of God fighting our battles and facing the enemy.

I worked on focusing on what God said about me rather than what my ex-husband said. I worked on not allowing how he treated me to define me. I felt the changes as I let go of the victim mentality and started living as a victor. I started putting God's word into action and saw jaw-dropping results. I also continued surrounding myself with strong relationships and friends who were supportive.

I know there may be someone reading this that is living with an abusive person. The fear and control can be paralyzing, leaving you to believe that you have no options. This is not true. There is help for you and your kids, but you have to take that first step. Go to your local police station or sheriff's office. They can help you take legal action and put you in contact with people who can help you.

If you don't feel safe going to the police, go to another person you trust who can help you break free. Reach out and let others help you. There are safe, private places where you can stay and get the help you need. You are the only one who can take control and get help for yourself and your kids.

Realizing you have the power to make that decision and follow through with it, brings about a new freedom you might've thought was impossible. Take hold of the fact that the Lord delights in you. He calls you by a new name, which is Hephzibah, "for the Lord will take delight you" Isaiah 62:4. He also says you shall be a "crown of splendor in the Lord's hand" Isaiah 62:3. You are precious to God. "Since you were precious in My sight you have been honored and I have loved you" Isaiah 43:4 (NKJ). He delights in you, you have a new name with Him and He holds you in His hand. You are precious and loved. God never intended for you to be abused.

When someone is betrayed or wronged, they can feel like a victim of circumstance. This may lead to a focus on the negatives in life rather than the positives, blaming the other party for the current problems while looking for pity. Validation is sought by hanging onto bitterness. I recognize this because I did it. I wanted those I confided in to feel sorry for me. I needed validation my feelings, and didn't realize I had succumbed to this victim mentality in a more subtle form.

That day as I talked with my pastor and realized I was living as a victim instead of a victorious Christian, was a definite marker in my walk with God. Even though I'd walked closely with Him, I saw how I needed to let go of so many things and pray to have His perspective. I'd also become comfortable in my junky thinking and had to step outside of that comfort zone before I could change. We have the power to choose if we're going to live our lives as victims or victors. Jesus Christ holds the key to this victory.

Today could be the beginning of the end of living as a victim of your circumstances. Do you want Jesus to unlock this new life for you? The first step is deciding you don't want to live this way anymore and admitting you are living as a victim. The next step is to read and study what God says about you. He has the power that you don't have to change you and your situation. You may not change the way you think and act immediately, but you will if you keep at it. Even though you may hate your present situation, this dysfunctional comfort zone could be what's keeping you from moving forward. Ask the Lord to reveal if this is what's holding you back.

The next thing is, if you feel it's necessary, seek godly counsel. Go to someone you trust and ask about support groups where you can meet others overcoming the similar issues. A recovery program such as Celebrate Recovery is a fantastic place to start. It's a Christ-centered program for anyone who struggles with a hurt, habit or hang-up and it's free. To find out more go to www.celebraterecovery.com. This is a safe place where you can remove the pretend mask and build a support system without any condemnation or being judged.

Finally, pray for a renewed mind as you study His word. The changes will be subtle at first, but soon you will begin to feel and act differently.

You don't have to live and think negatively anymore. This is not what God wants for you. He wants to free you from victimization and put you on the path to victorious freedom. Don't wait another day. Join Him in the process right now by taking the first step.

"With God we will gain the victory, and he will trample down our enemies" Psalm 60:12.

Marker Ten: From the Battlefield to the Sanctuary

We face battles every day, don't we? Some are more intense than others. There have been raging battles that have left me weary to the point of giving up. God has always used music to lift me out of the dumps after a battle, to bring me into His sanctuary where I find strength to go back out again. Something powerful happens when we praise God with scriptural songs and music that overcomes the work of the enemy.

When my daughter turned thirteen, she wanted to go live with her dad. Living with her father would mean an unstable environment where there were few boundaries and rules. At that time he had a large house with an in-ground pool and all the freedom a teenager could want. I never dreamed in a million years I'd come to this road. This also transpired during the time I was preparing for the Honduras mission trip.

I remember sitting on the front porch of that same little "cracker-jack box" house crying to God saying, "Lord, I don't know what to do. What would *You* do?" I'd already been down this road with my son and it was a terrible mistake to let him go. After asking God that question, a quiet voice deep in my heart spoke in an immediate response saying, "I wouldn't allow **MY** daughter to live over there."

Even though she had an earthly father, God is her ultimate Father and has the final say. I knew then, I had to take action. I also knew this wasn't a battle I could fight on my own, and knew God's Word had a lot to say about Him fighting our battles. I immediately began searching the Bible on this subject. I'm not a fighter by nature and hate confrontation. God enabled me to stand my ground and when her father realized I was going to fight, things intensified and became even more difficult. This ultimately led to the most victorious, mind-blowing chain of events, leaving no room for doubt in the power of God's Word and the power of praising Him with song and music.

In the state where I live, when children are fourteen, they have a choice to live with either parent. To fight for custody of a thirteen-year old seemed a waste of time and money, especially when she already wanted to go. All I knew was what God had said to me that day on the porch. The environment she would be going to was unstable and could change without warning. I put off discussing it with her in hopes that the issue would die down. Things finally came to a head by the end of the summer. The conviction I felt in my heart drove me to fight and stand in front of a judge, seemingly wasting everyone's time and money.

The judge reminded me that my daughter would soon be fourteen, and asked why I was spending the time and money to pursue this. He didn't know all the circumstances surrounding her father's life, so I just looked foolish. I knew God would not take me down this road without providing what I needed to continue on in the fight. As I turned to His word for direction and comfort, I discovered that all I was required to do was take my place, stand still and watch to see what the Lord would do.

"And Moses said to the people, 'Do not be afraid. Stand still, and see the salvation of the Lord, which He will accomplish for you today. For the Egyptians whom you see today, you shall see again no more forever. The Lord will fight for you, and you shall hold your peace' " Exodus 14:13-14 (NKJ). I stood on this promise, even when my stomach was in knots and I lost a lot of sleep.

During this time I studied the events found in II Chronicles 20:1-24. It's a story about God fighting on behalf of the people of Judah that became the model through which I operated as God led me through this battle. As God enabled me to respond as the people of Judah did, I saw Him work in ways I couldn't even have thought possible.

Several different armies were waging war against the people of Judah. Their leader, Jehoshaphat, cried out to God in distress. He was confident that God would hear him and save them. God promised they wouldn't have to fight the battle, but instructed them to move forward toward the battlefield, take their positions and stand firm. He assured them they would be delivered. They were instructed through their leader, Jehoshaphat, that song and praise should lead all the people of Judah into battle. As they marched onward, they sang, "Give thanks to the Lord, for His love endures forever" II Chronicles 20:21. As they sang God's praises, He set up ambushes against their enemies, who started fighting among themselves, eventually killing each other until no one was left. When Jehoshaphat and his army approached the battlefield, they saw that all their enemies were dead. They went in and collected their possessions without even having to fight in the battle.

That one sentence, "Give thanks to the Lord, for His love endures forever," became my anthem. At first I felt silly singing those words as I approached my ex-husband's house each time. But then I started noticing that he no longer came out to the car to confront me each time I pulled in the driveway when picking up or dropping off our daughter. I held my position and didn't budge. I acted just like the Israelites when Moses encouraged them in Exodus 13:14, and the people of Judah in II Chronicles 20. It wasn't I who won, but God.

In the end we came to a joint-custody agreement. While I agreed to the new custody arrangement, I still sensed God wasn't finished with this battle. Because of the years of instability and the choices my ex-husband continued to make, I believed that God's intention was to grant me full custody of our daughter. As I left the courthouse that last day of court proceedings, I remember saying to the Lord, "This cannot be Your best solution. I know You aren't finished yet." I left the remaining process in His hands and waited to see what happened next.

Within several days, before the papers hit the judge's desk for signature, my ex-husband's life went out of control. The chain of events that unfolded left me speechless. Along with his third divorce and the surrounding circumstances, I watched my daughter do a 180-degree turn around while God grabbed hold of her heart. I called my attorney to have the custody papers withdrawn. At the end of all these events right before turning fourteen, she legally remained under my custody. She no longer acted as though she hated me. About a year later told me I was only doing what any parent should do. We didn't talk much about that awful time. I just stood and watched God work, just as He had directed me to do in Exodus 14:13.

God met me in this marker: His word is powerful and satan's schemes and plots cannot stand against it. I don't understand what happened in the heavens or spiritual realm when I sang those words each time I faced a battle, but it worked. There is power in our praise and worship to God in the midst of the assaults. When the battlefield leaves you weary, you can enter God's presence through songs of praise. Every time you come from the battlefield into His sanctuary you will find strength and power to go back out again and again. Coming to Him every day will prepare you and protect you while the battle rages.

What are you facing today? God will never bring us to a battle without providing the weapons needed to withstand and overcome. One of those weapons is entering His sanctuary confidently through praise and worship. Praise Him with your battle songs. You don't have to wait until Sunday morning when the music starts. You can start right where you are, right now.

"The Lord will fight for you; you need only to be still" Exodus 14:14.

Marker Eleven: Treasures of Darkness

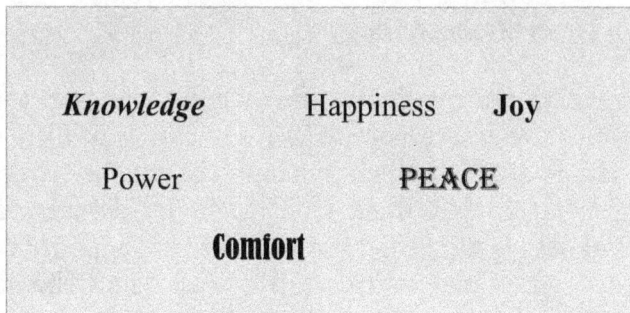

Knowledge   Happiness   **Joy**

Power   **PEACE**

Comfort

We have come quite a ways together by now. I hope that you have a fresh, new perspective on how active and personal God is in your life. He wants you to know that He will go before you and make the crooked places straight. If someone had told me twenty years ago I'd be writing and sharing my past heartaches and hardships with you, I wouldn't have believed them. As the years have unfolded, an increasing desire and passion has risen out of my hardships and sorrows, as God has given me the desire to write. If someone had told me I'd be remarried and finishing these last two sections sitting in my favorite place in the world, I would've never thought that possible.

It's 6:30 a.m. I'm listening to the ocean waves crashing outside on St. George Island, Florida. My husband and I come here to enjoy the slow, relaxing pace and beauty of this small island. We can take a step back in time as God uses this place to refresh us. The past 23 years prepared me for this time.

God used the experiences of pain and hardship to lead me to the man I married. He feels the same way. He recently said, "it builds you into a different person." My husband has seen his fair share of darkness throughout his life and is the man he is today because of them. He is allowing Christ to turn his past pain and darkness into treasures and riches that have no price tag. He is an example to me of pressing through and allowing God to change those dark times into lasting treasures.

God will bring the richest gems out of your darkness. You don't have to look far, but you do have to keep your eyes open. "I will give you the treasures of darkness and hidden riches of secret places, that you may know that I, the Lord, Who call you by your name, am the God of Israel" Isaiah 45:3 (NKJ).

After reading the previous verse, what do treasures and riches mean to you? A treasure is priceless, something of high value. We think of riches as that which can only be attained with limitless resources. What do you think God means by darkness and secret places? Darkness is the difficult times and hardships we experience. It can also be the times when we live in sin and rebellion against God. For me personally, the secret place is when I am completely alone, it's quiet, dark, and no one but God is there. It's in that very secret place of the heart that only He knows and has the ability and power to reach.

Isaiah 45 was written about Cyrus, the king of Persia. Cyrus was an anointed instrument of God who did more for God's people than most of the kings of Israel and Judah. You and I are also anointed. "But you have an anointing from the Holy One, and all of you know the truth" I John 2:20. If you've received Jesus Christ as your Savior and Lord, then He's given you His Spirit of anointing to live out your Christian life and accomplish the things He's planned for you. He has great plans for you and it is never too late.

When we enter times of suffering, our first response is to ask God why. We might assume it means we're going in the wrong direction. We might blame God and question why this happening if He is such a loving God. It is in those times of suffering and darkness that we can experience the goodness of God. I know that without all the difficult, painful times I've walked through, I wouldn't know the mercy and grace of God the way I now do. If my life had been without the trials, I would not have experienced His power and provision as I trusted His word and followed Him through it all.

He uses our dark times to show us His power. Nothing in this world can do what the power of God can. It's through our suffering that we learn to relate to Christ. He suffered the worst, possible betrayal and physical pain, yet in that hour of darkness, the greatest treasure in history and incomparable riches were gained. He did it for you and me. So the suffering we may endure here on earth can't be compared to the eternal joy we'll experience with Him forever.

But while we wait for that, He will give us treasures and riches here on earth that cannot be bought and will never be found in the world.

One of these great treasures is joy. Finding joy in the midst of your suffering is nothing short of a miracle. You can't get it from the world. Joy isn't a feeling that comes and goes when your circumstances change. Joy is a reality you experience as you trust God in the midst of your heartache and pain. God's joy is also found during the good times, but you still have to search for it. If things are going well for you right now, your joy may not be God-given but rather a result of this trouble-free zone. His joy comes to the heart that seeks Him in good times and bad.

Comfort is another wonderful treasure. You can have a comfortable life that's based on financial security and healthy relationships. Any of these things can change abruptly or be taken without warning. The comfort that the Holy Spirit provides during dark times is priceless. This is the kind of comfort that II Corinthians I, 3-4 addresses. "Praise be to the God and Father of our Lord Jesus Christ, the Father of compassion and the God of all comfort, who comforts us in all our troubles, so that we can comfort those in any trouble with the comfort we ourselves receive from God."

The world offers temporary contentment. Worldly contentment that's based on circumstances can change like shifting wind. Contentment that comes from God is based on the truths and promises of His Word no matter your circumstances. This type of contentment is linked with joy and comfort. "The fear of the Lord leads to life: Then one rests content, untouched by trouble" Proverbs 19:23. This doesn't mean you won't have trouble, but that you'll rest content through your troubles. "Untouched by trouble" means you'll come out the victor in the end.

Paul stated in Philippians 4:12-13, "I know what it is to be in need, and I know what it is to have plenty. I have learned the secret of being content in any and every situation, whether well fed or hungry, whether living in plenty or in want. I can do everything through him who gives me strength." Paul's secret rested in his focus and knowing where his strength came from. When our focus shifts to me, myself, and I, and all our problems, we fall into discontent, which ultimately leads to misery.

Do you think the world offers peace? Surely not these days! I truthfully don't know how anyone makes it today without being in relationship with Jesus Christ. There is nothing the world can offer us in the way of peace. Real peace can only come from being in a personal relationship with God, through Jesus Christ. He is the only one who can give peace that passes all understanding even in the midst of these times in which we live.

You may have found other treasures as you've walked through dark times. Some of those may be treasures of forgiveness, mercy, grace and thankfulness, just to name a few. The list could go on and on. The treasure chest is full, but you have to unlock it, open it and take possession of theses treasures. If our lives were always easy, would we even be motived to look for them? The road I traveled as a single mom was very difficult and painful at times. At the same time, it was also very rich and full of treasures. It still amazes me even as I share this with you!

Above all these treasures is wisdom and knowledge we receive from Christ through His Word. "Oh, the depth of the riches both of the wisdom and knowledge of God" Romans 11:33, and "…namely, Christ, in whom are hidden all the treasures of wisdom and knowledge" Colossians 2:2-3. According to Proverbs 2:1-4, we're to search for wisdom and knowledge as if we're searching for hidden treasure.

What do you think you need to embark on this great treasure hunt? You need a map! Thankfully the Lord has provided. "If any of you lacks wisdom, he should ask God, who gives generously to all without finding fault, and it will be given to him. But when he asks, he must believe and not doubt, because he who doubts is like a wave of the sea, blown and tossed by the wind" James 1:5-6. If you are searching for treasures and riches in a man, job, financial security or anything else that can be taken away, stop looking and go back to your map. Start seeking the treasures and riches God has for you right now.

What is your story? What have you experienced that God can use for His glory? What do you think He wants to do with your heartaches and hardships? What treasures do you think you will find along the way as you trust His leading? God won't waste anything if you give it to Him to use. You don't have to wait until things get better or you meet some great guy. You don't have to wait until you have enough money or the house you've always wanted. Those are all things that can be taken away or never given. You can have all of God's treasures and riches right now. They won't come through a dream house, dream man or dream job. When you find His priceless, enduring treasures, nothing and no one can take them away.

These days my life might look easy to someone else. I married a wonderful man and don't have the same financial worries. I have a comfortable home I share with my husband, and a decent job that allows me the flexibility to take off and enjoy these beach getaways. Even with these new provisions, there are still heartaches I deal with every day because of the past. I have to give those to God every day. I have to be intentional in not worrying about my grown kids and the deep repercussions of the past. My son turned thirty at the time of this writing and I hadn't seen him in over a year. My heart aches, yet at the same time I put my hope in God. This is where I find comfort. I know that one day our relationship will be renewed and restored. (Another book for another time).

We all have internal struggles. It seems there is constantly something that needs addressing in my life. Just because I'm writing this to you, doesn't mean I have all the answers without any more struggles. We will always have trials and obstacles to overcome in this life. Living also includes victory, joy, peace, contentment, and closeness with God. These alone bring the happiness we all crave.

While I know the things I have today can be taken away tomorrow, I can say with confidence the treasures I've gained in the darkness will never be taken from me. I would not have these treasures if it hadn't been for the darkness. I strive to live every day with a thankful heart, knowing that God gives and God takes away. He will never take away His treasures and riches that are discovered in the darkness.

Let this be a concrete marker for you: Hold on tightly to what God provides through your struggles and dark times. Hold on loosely to the things you gain from the world, knowing they could be taken at any time. Don't expect to gain all these treasures and riches overnight. DO expect to find them one by one as you diligently search and dig. Open up the treasure chest of what is in your possession. One day soon, you will realize that you have become a very rich woman!

"I will give you the treasures of darkness, riches stored in secret places, so that you may know that I am the LORD, the God of Israel, who summons you by name" Isaiah 45:3.

Marker Twelve: Pressing On

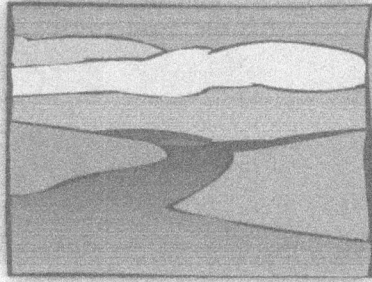

The journey continues and God never stops giving guidance and direction. There are many more markers to guide me on the path God has for me. I hope you've discovered some of the markers God has used in your life to provide direction. I pray you've come to know how passionate the Lord's love is for you and how precious you are to Him. My desire is that you've been able to begin letting go of those things which are behind, and start reaching forward to those things which are ahead (Philippians 3:13). I know you can't completely forget, but you can begin the process of letting go of the past. Easier said than done, right? If it were easy we could do it on our own and wouldn't need God to get us there. This is why I say, "beginning the process." It's a lifelong process.

Paul, in Philippians Chapter 3, makes it clear that none of us ever fully arrive perfected while we're here on this earth. But we can press on into our future with God by letting go of those things that are behind and reaching forward, constantly moving upward with God, and walking in the life He has for us. It's very hard to let go of the past. Hurts, bad habits and terrible hang-ups are the very things that throw us to the ground and sit on top of us.

Paul tells us in Galatians 5, "It is for freedom that Christ has set us free. Stand firm then and do not let yourselves be burdened again by a yoke of slavery." In other words, stand strong in the freedom you have with Christ and don't let sin hold you back any longer from moving forward with Him. Paul is talking about all sin here, including unforgiveness, bitterness, anger and all the things that we hang onto following a divorce or other hurts involving relationships.

You don't necessarily forget completely. Our minds don't work that way. However you can get to the place where your painful memories don't hold you back from moving forward. Ironically, they can be the very tool God uses to catapult you forward into the new life He has for you. He plans to use you and your story in others' lives. So maybe that's why we don't completely forget.

Bad habits and hang-ups don't just go away with time. They are what we pack in our bags and carry through life with us. Getting married after nineteen years as a single mom, I soon discovered I had some unpacking to do. There were things I just didn't have to deal with while I was single. Now that I'm married, God is always showing me things I need to remove and toss out of my bags. For someone who likes to travel light, I've had to do a lot of unpacking. I think it's going to take me the rest of my life, but at least my luggage is getting lighter. I hope to move to a backpack soon, and then a shoulder bag.

It took me a long time to get over the hurt and pain of my divorce and all the before and after stuff that came with it. I wasn't able to walk away from my first marriage easily, as I held onto the hope that my husband would come back, even after the divorce. I struggled with forgiving and forgetting as well as with my own issues. These weren't just a result of the painful end of my marriage, but also life-long hang-ups, which no doubt contributed to the demise of my marriage.

It wasn't until I finally accepted that I couldn't change anyone else, but could only change myself with God's strength, that I began to move on. I can still remember the moment I decided that the Lord alone should be my focus. This was the one relationship in which I could grow deeper and stronger. I knew that Jesus would never leave me.

I began to press on with God and not worry about what others did anymore. I didn't hear thunder or see lightning bolts. I was in my kitchen when this revelation came to me. I let it all go and remember feeling the first bit of emotional relief in a very long time. It was in that moment that II Corinthians 1:3-4 became a reality to me. "Praise be to the God and Father of our Lord Jesus Christ, the Father of compassion and the God of all comfort, who comforts us in all our troubles, so that we can comfort those in any trouble with the comfort we ourselves have received from God." That's when I realized everything I'd been through in the past or would experience in the future would not be wasted. God would use it if I let Him.

Of course, there have been too many times to count that I've had to re-release things to God, but He's always right there to take it again and again. There have been too many times to count that I've fallen and failed, but He's always right there, patiently waiting to let Him pick me back up again.

I wish I could say I've been consistent and didn't feel like I've failed my kids or made mistakes, but it wouldn't be true. There are many things I'm still waiting to see God accomplish, things I have no control over. I continue to pray, hope and wait. I don't doubt the stable, active power of God's mercy, grace and compassion in people's lives, including mine.

Whatever you've endured, it is all part of what God will use to strengthen you and bring purpose to your life. "But the Lord is faithful, and He will strengthen you and protect you from the evil one" II Thessalonians 3:3. Don't you want to be strengthened and protected from the evil one? Ask God to enable you to let go of all that keeps you from having that with Him. Whether it's sin in your life, a bad habit or life-long hang-ups, nothing is too difficult for Him.

If you are dealing with a serious habit or issue that you need help with, once again, I strongly encourage you to seek out the nearest Celebrate Recovery program. This powerful Christ-centered recovery program involves people just like you and me who need help letting go of painful pasts and damaging habits that keep us from living the Spirit-filled life God intended. Here's the website again: www.celebraterecovery.com.

A promise I've held onto all these years is found in I Peter 5:30. "But may the God of all grace, who called us to His eternal glory by Christ Jesus, after you have suffered a while, perfect, establish, strengthen, and settle you" (NKJ). Our sufferings here on earth can't begin to compare to the eternity we will spend with Jesus. Our minds aren't designed to fully comprehend this. I believe it also means that He is working today to perfect, establish, strengthen and settle you, today, as you walk through this life.

God has brought stability to my life that I used to only dream about. Whether married, single, healthy, sick or alone, my security is wrapped up in who God is through my relationship with Jesus. In an effort to find happiness, we sometimes wallow in our regrets and self-pity with hope of finding comfort there. As the wise analysis of my husband clearly states, "I've tried that, and found out it doesn't work."

I regret a lot of things. I'll never regret giving my heart to Jesus, surrendering and abandoning my life to Him and trusting Him. To this day I don't regret my decision to let go of people and circumstances I have no control over. I don't regret that day in my kitchen when I decided to move on with God. Maintaining regrets takes a lot more energy than simply letting go of something you can't change anyway. The truth is the only thing I really have control over is my attitude and relying on God to do His work in me.

What about you? Are you traveling through your life with loaded baggage? It's a heavy load, isn't it? All your regrets, hurtful betrayals, past sins, hang-ups and bad habits leave no room for new things. I like new things. I've never met a woman yet who didn't like new things. Out with the old, in with the new is the saying. "Therefore, if anyone is in Christ, he is a new creation; the old has gone, the new has come" II Corinthians 5:17! Are you going to walk in the new or the old? What will your redemptive story be? What path will you take? Which markers will you follow?

Be encouraged with the words in Romans 6:4. "We were therefore buried with Him through baptism into death in order that, just as Christ was raised from the dead through the glory of the Father, we too may live a new life."

Now, go and live your new life!

"Brethren, I do not count myself to have apprehended, but one thing I do, forgetting those things which are behind and reaching forward to those things which are ahead. I press toward the goal for

the prize of the upward call of God in Christ Jesus," Philippians 3:13-14 (NKJ).

P.S. Now that you've started a new life, you must have a new name. What will it be? Remember reading in Marker 9 what God says your new name is? "The Gentiles shall see your righteousness, and all kings your glory. You shall be called by a new name, which the mouth of the Lord will name. You shall also be a crown of glory in the hand of the Lord, and a royal diadem in the hand of your God. You shall no longer be termed Forsaken, nor shall your land anymore be called Desolate; but you shall be called Hephzibah (My delight is in her) and your land Beulah (married), for the Lord delights in you" Isaiah 62:2-4.

I'm praying you walk in the knowledge of who you are, His chosen one, given a new name by the God who loves you, a royal jewel in His hand!

Marker Thirteen: The Tree

All these stories of mine really aren't my stories. They're God's stories. He's the writer. As He has been writing His story through my life all these years, I am sure He's wanted to throw His hands up, yell or pull His hair out (if God has hair). I can be dense, slow, stubborn and self-centered most of the time. As one who journals (with pen and paper), I get frustrated when a pen runs out of ink, doesn't write anymore. Maybe I should invest in nice fountain pens.

I see myself as a fountain pen that God is trying to use to write His story. I run out of ink, leave blobs of ink behind or the ink simply dries up and is of no use. He'll refill the pen (me), then the words will flow again, bringing Him pleasure, as the story continues coming together in His way. I believe God sees all, hears all and knows all. Sometimes I wonder, though, if He's had to search for that fountain pen (me) because I was trying to hide or get lost. I'm curious if God ever gets frustrated like I do when looking for a pen and can't find one, especially when it's one I love to write with.

During the years when we lived in that "cracker-jack box" house I mentioned in Marker 7, God continually amazed me in the midst of some of our most dire circumstances. We moved into that house about a year after returning from our three months with the mission organization in Hawaii. I was working full time at the technical college, which was a 40-mile commute one way. My son had gone to live with his father, so it was just my daughter and me. We moved into that house around Christmas of 1994. The following summer was one of the hottest in Georgia. The rusted, old Ford Tempo I was driving had no air conditioning and neither did the house. The attic fan brought some relief at night and thankfully we were gone during the day.

Towards the end of the summer of '95, someone gave us two window air-conditioners. Bill Davenport, a very sweet and generous man from my small group, sold me a car for $1. It was a white Geo Metro with air conditioning that we named Snowball. That car never broke down or left me stranded! I also called it my God car. Since Bill's in heaven now, I hope he knows how much that car ministered to me and my kids.

When things were bad, God would show up. He used my church family and friends in ways I will never be able to express in words. Even though things were very tough, I was surrounded and hugely blessed with great friends who loved us, prayed for us and accepted us. This is why I urge you to find a healthy church home, where you can plant, root and grow.

Since I was renting this house, I was responsible for all the yard work. It was an older house, so the bushes and trees were well established and quite large. The overgrown, red-tip bushes had to be trimmed often and the half-acre of grass kept cut. In the middle of the front yard stood a massive sweet-gum-ball tree that I had a love-hate relationship with. In the summer it was grand, providing shade for the whole front yard and most of the house (remember, we had no central air). In the fall, it dropped bazillions of those prickly little balls and all its leaves. When I'd cut the grass in the summer all those dead prickly balls would shoot through the push lawn mower making the most awful noise. My next-door neighbor would peek over his fence and watch, adding to the discomfort I was already experiencing.

One day I came home from work to find people in my front yard. Someone was on a ladder trimming the very bushy bushes, and the lawn was being mowed and raked. When I finally closed my dropped jaw from the surprise and went into the house, people were inside cleaning, mopping and sweeping. Usually when these unexpected blessings would occur, it was because someone instigated it, organized it and followed through with the mission. I won't mention any names, but her name started with an "S" and ended with an "E". It was the same girl who, years prior strongly encouraged me to join that nine-month Bible study with her. God sure knew what He was doing when he replaced my old best friend with this new best friend, who still today sticks with me like glue.

It was while living in this house that I pined away for those months spent with YWAM (the mission organization) in Hawaii. I missed all my new friends which were now scattered around the world. We kept in touch with letters and phone calls, and I even got to visit a few of them who lived in nearby states. I was, I believe, also suffering the consequences of not continuing on with the whole class and completing the outreach phase of my training. I was constantly dealing with a broken lawn mower, washing machine, vacuum cleaner, car or something.

I had a lot of peaceful times in that house though. Even though my ex-husband and his new wife (my old best friend) had bought a five-bedroom home, in an upscale neighborhood, I had something they didn't. Peace. I had the Arm of God. When I pulled into my driveway and walked through the kitchen door, God's presence met me there. It took me a while to see that.

I learned that things weren't always as they appeared to the outside world. My ex-husband's marriage with my old best friend lasted two years. She left him for his friend and business partner. I don't share that because it made me feel good when it happened. I was over the pain and heartache by the time they married. I share it because if you've been hurt and betrayed, and there appears to be no justice, things will ultimately change. God hasn't turned away from your situation. Continue to stay in right relationship with the Lord. He's a just God. He's also a forgiving God, and if my ex-husband and friend truly turn to Him for forgiveness, repent and give their lives to Him, then God will forgive them. I'm no different in my need for God's forgiveness. None of us are.

My favorite place of this little house was the concrete front porch. The roof of the house extended over the porch and was supported by two round columns. The overgrown bushes provided privacy from the street and on either side of my porch, so neighbors couldn't see when I sat in my wooden rocker. I spent a great deal of time on that porch, staring into nowhere, praying, reading, journaling. I complained to God a lot while sitting that front porch. That's where He told me not to let my daughter go live with her father when she thought that's what she wanted.

I also had a lot of great times on that porch. Eye-opening talks with God; times with Him that left me feeling hugged and protected. There were many talks with another bestie, Susan, the friend I'd asked God for. I asked Him to bring another single mom into my life who could tell me how to do it right. So He brings Susan, a single mom sixteen years older than me, but every bit as young. Because of her unyielding surrender to the Lord, she has served in local and foreign mission projects, traveling to places I only dream of. She's been a part of some incredible God-sized projects. As I mentioned on my dedication page of this book, I learned grace and strength from Susan. She's the big sister I always wanted.

After a long day of hot, sweaty yard work, the rocking chair on that front porch was my resting place usually accompanied by a big glass of iced-tea. It was my early morning spot with a hot cup of coffee.

One day, as I sat on my front porch, I complained to God. I hated my life most of the time. I hated my circumstances. I hated my commute to work and didn't even enjoy my job that much. I hated living in that town where my ex-husband was still trying to control me, using the kids as pawns on a chessboard. I was tired of being broke and feeling broken. I complained to God about how much I hated living there, asked why do I have to live here, blah, blah, blah.

Then as sure as I am typing these words, I heard Him say, ever so gently and quietly to my heart, "Do you see that big old tree there in the front yard?" You couldn't miss that tree which I loved and hated. I answered Him, "Yes, I see it." Next came this, which I didn't expect at all. "You see how the roots of that tree spread across parts of the yard and obviously grow so deep down that the tree can't be uprooted?" I already had a feeling of what was coming next. He wasn't going to tell me I could start packing because I was getting out of this hell hole. He said, "I'm going to root you and ground you just like that tree. I want you to set roots and grow where I've planted you."

I didn't know if that meant I had to live there forever, but in any case, He answered me in response to "why do I have to live here!" God spoke! And it made sense! I didn't particularly like His answer, but I knew it was Him. I couldn't even think up something like that. I also knew, despite all I'd gone through, that He had a purpose for everything and that ONE day it would all make sense. In case you're wondering, we lived in that house four-and-a-half years.

In the middle of all the years of being a single mom, a dream and vision for ministry to single parents had taken root. Deep down it gnawed at me, but I just couldn't imagine how God would ever bring it to reality. How could I help someone else when it seemed my life was always such a mess? Despite that, the vision grew through the years as I continually endured struggles and hardships. Because of all I'd been through, and how God had met me day after mundane day, I not only saw the demand for such a ministry, but knew first-hand what hard-working, struggling single parents truly needed.

The truth is, God never let me down!! He never failed to provide as long as I'd stay out of the way. When I'd let Him be my Father and Husband, and stop acting like a fatherless child or complaining wife, He did His greatest work, continually writing His story on the pages of my life.

The Lord was always faithful in providing employment, but I lived one paycheck away from eviction most of the time. Scraping up enough change to put gas in my car the day before payday was normal. I don't have a college degree, so my career choices were minimal and salary matched my education. I had a high school diploma, a few college courses under my belt, and secretarial skills and experience that kept me employed.

Without dragging this out, fast forward about fifteen years. Spring Ministries, a single-parent ministry, is being penned by God. The ink is fresh, pen in His hand and He continues writing. The ministry vision always included a transitional home with a wrap-around porch. Single moms would come there to find rest and reside temporarily while they rebuild their lives after an uprooting event such as divorce or death of a spouse. Perhaps they may have never married, but suddenly find themselves in this role with little or no support. Spring would be the place for the hard-working single mom who just needs a break and a little bit of help to get her back on her feet.

Spring stands for Single Parents Rooted in New Ground. This is based on Isaiah 61:3, "To console those who mourn in Zion, to give them beauty for ashes, the oil of joy for mourning, the garment of praise for the spirit of heaviness, that they may be called trees of righteousness, the planting of the Lord, that He may be gloried." The single mom and her children would live in this place while she pursued or finished her education, became employed and received financial, spiritual and emotional counseling. She would learn how to save and purchase her own home. She would not receive handouts without accountability that would keep her in a cycle of despair. She would be surrounded by people who will help her and her children UP and OUT.

There would be car care maintenance, clothes for work, child care, career counseling, support groups, friendships formed, and new lives with new names. Her children would witness the expression of who Jesus is through practical helps and hands-on involvement. Because of that they will grow up to know Him, becoming productive in their community. This vision included wooden rockers on the wrap-around porch and places to sit and rest. This is where they will plan their future, get re-rooted, planted, and grow, and so much more.

God is still writing, but I can tell you now, there is a place being prepared. I can't say exactly how it will all play out. This place has lots and lots of trees around it, a completely covered, wrap-around deck with plenty of room for those rockers and outdoor quiet times, fellowship, or just sitting alone and resting. Maybe that's another book God will write, of how He brings all this into reality. Little 'ol me hasn't the brains or energy to create what God is creating for Spring Ministries. I can't count the number of people who have donated time, money, furniture and supplies, resources, hard labor in painting, construction, repairs, nice clothes, and prayed for us, and on and on His story goes.

Are you letting God write His story through your life? Writers often talk about "rewrites". Can God rewrite your story? Will you be the ink in His pen? God will fulfill all His promises to you. Let Him write the markers for your life.

That big old tree became a huge marker in my life. God is currently unfolding how He is fulfilling what He said that day to me on the concrete porch. Only He and He alone can accomplish this.

As I said in the beginning of my letter to you, I'm not anymore special or deserving than the next person. God isn't looking for people who are smarter, more educated, more spiritual or more capable. He just wants people who are AVAILABLE. Will you make your life available to Him? He's the one who is able. I can't think of a better way to complete this part of His story, than this:

Ephesians 3:14-21 "For this reason I kneel before the Father, from whom every family in heaven and on earth derives its name, I pray that out of his glorious riches he may strengthen you with power through his Spirit in your inner being, so that Christ may dwell in your hearts through faith. And I pray that you, being rooted and established in love, may have power, together with all the Lord's holy people, to grasp how wide and long and high and deep is the love of Christ, and to know this love that surpasses knowledge—that you may be filled to the measure of all the fullness of God. Now to him who is able to do immeasurably more than all we ask or imagine, according to his power that is at work within us, to him be glory in the church and in Christ Jesus throughout all generations, for ever and ever! Amen.

About the Author

Terri Webster

As an author and blogger, Terri encourages and inspires readers to stay the course, win their individual race, as described by Paul in Hebrews 12:1 in the Bible. She uses the spiritual markers God has placed in her life, as guidance along her path, and strives to spur others to recognize the unique spiritual markers God is using in their life.

"We are all on a unique journey, tailored especially for us. No one's marked course is like anyone else's. It's about staying the course and running the race that Jesus has only for you."

Terri also published When All Seems Lost: Prayer Markers for Finding Your Way, a small prayer book to guide readers through sorrow and loss.

Keep an outlook for her upcoming novel: To the Forgotten Coast: Journey from Bitter, Cold Loss to the Balmy Shores of Sweet Redemption, due to publish in the Fall of 2019.

She's a contributor to Chicken for the Soul and Pens in the Piedmont.

Join her at https://womeninneedwin.blogspot.com/

www.ingramcontent.com/pod-product-compliance
Lightning Source LLC
Chambersburg PA
CBHW020512030426
42337CB00011B/347